D0330129

ANCHOR

God's Promises of Hope to Parents

ANCHOR

God's Promises of Hope to Parents

JAMES B. STENSON

Scepter

Other books by James B. Stenson, published by Scepter Publishers

Compass: A Handbook on Parent Leadership

Lifeline: The Religious Upbringing of Your Children

Preparing for Adolescence: A Planning Guide for Parents

Preparing for Peer Pressure: A Guide for Parents of Young Children

Successful Fathers: The Subtle but Powerful Ways Fathers Mold Their Children's Characters

Upbringing: A Discussion Handbook for Parents of Young Children

Father: The Family Protector

Published by Scepter Publishers, Inc., New York, N.Y. 10018
(800) 322–8773 / www.scepterpublishers.org

First printing April 2003
Second printing November 2003
Third printing April 2006

ISBN 1–889334–82–0

Text composition in ITC Cheltenham Book

Printed in the United States of America

Contents

Introduction

Dear Friend,

This little book is all about hope. It is about your hope in God and his hope in you.

It describes the resplendent light and power God gives to men and women when he calls them to their holy mission of parenthood. It lays out the promises God makes to parents when he entrusts them with their children's souls—and counts on them to lead their children to a great life here on earth and then life with him forever.

I have called this work *Anchor* for a reason.

From the earliest age of the Church, the anchor has been a symbol of hope for Christians. It was scratched on the graves of early Christian martyrs. It has ever been a sign of Christ's protection through the storms of life to those who love him. The Epistle to the Hebrews (6:19) says of Christ, "We have this as a sure and steadfast anchor of the soul. . . . "

St. Paul knew a few things about storms and shipwrecks. In his famous litany of the travails he endured for Christ (2 Cor 11:23–30), he mentions being shipwrecked three times. In yet another sea-storm off the shores of Malta, he nearly perished; but he and the ship were saved just in time by the protective force of anchors. St. Luke, his companion on the journey, described this event vividly in Acts 27: "Then fearing that we might run on the rocks, they let out four anchors from the stern, and prayed for day to come."

You too have an anchor that gives salvation to your mission. That anchor is the faith and hope you have in God, who protects you and your family as his tenderly beloved children.

This book is, in a sense, a companion and sequel to *Lifeline: The Religious Upbringing of Your Children*. In that work, I described how Christian parents—men and women just like you—manage to bring up their children right, that is, how they lead their children to God and a great life. It outlined a job description, if you will, of the vocation to parenthood.

But as you know, this task of raising children takes years of patient, sometimes valiant, effort. It calls for holding on through roller-coaster ups and downs, reverses and triumphs, ongoing challenges that can strain your stamina and patience and peace of mind. To persevere through all of this, you need the anchor of hope—of *the* Hope, of Christ himself.

So I've written *Anchor* for you: for your confidence and peace of mind. *Anchor* says to you, in effect, "Hang in there! It's worth it. You are doing God's will, and so he smiles on you. He trusts you, blesses you, and will never fail you. This he promised."

Because you are so busy, I have made this book brief and straight to the point. As you can see with a glance through its pages, its format is not that of a text or treatise. Rather, I have collected bits of hope-filled advice and encouragement from many sources, above all the Scriptures. These I have configured in a pithy, point-by-point way—like the counsels you'd receive from a spiritual director.

This is the format you would find in other spiritual works: the *Didache* of the ancient Church, the matchless *Imitation of Christ* by Thomas à Kempis, and the luminous works of St. Josemaría Escrivá directed to busy laypeople (*The Way*, *Furrow*, and *The Forge*). I do not claim that *Anchor* stands on the high spiritual plane of these other works. But my intention is the same: to give you ideas to read and reread over the course of years, to think and pray about from time to time, as reminders of your mission, sources for your hope, inspirations to your perseverance.

I should say here that the core spirituality of *Anchor* derives from that of St. Josemaría Escrivá, the founder of Opus Dei, whose holy life and teachings inspire countless parents to the love and service of God in normal life. As a priest, he has been a spiritual father to millions, including me. I owe him the gratitude of a son.

In January of 2001, Pope John Paul II—another great spiritual father—addressed a milestone Apostolic Letter to the whole Church, both for now and through the centuries to come. In this work, "Setting Forth into the New Millennium," the Holy Father laid out God's blueprint for the Church's next missionary expansion throughout the world: personal holiness. Not only piety, not only a good life, but holiness itself. He set plainly as a course of action what the Second Vatican Counsel taught: We are all called to be saints—to be the kind of men and women who, with souls enkindled by the Holy Spirit, will renew the face of the earth.

Holiness, nothing less. This is what God calls you to. This is what God wills for your children. And this is what *Anchor* is all about.

The book is divided into four chapters. The first three follow from a stirring and beautiful passage about vocation in the Book of Jeremiah that should stand as a guidepost on your journey. These three chapters explore the following three ideas: your divine vocation, your life of prayer with God, and your faithful perseverance to final triumph.

I have saved the best, though, for the fourth chapter, the passages from the Old and New Testaments in which God speaks to you, heart to heart, about the splendid adventure of your calling. There you will find God's promises to you, your anchor of hope now and in the years to come.

1.

Your Sacred Mission as a Parent

If you wish to understand the sublime reality of your vocation from God, his mission to you as a parent, you may begin by doing this: Return to the time of your childhood, that age when this world filled you with wonder, and look at the nighttime sky the way you did as a child. We adults, from time to time, need to see life as children see it—which is the way God sees it—a gift of wondrous beauty and a call to adventure.

When we lift our eyes to the heavens on a clear, cloudless night, we see the swirl of stars God flung across the endless expanse of the universe. And if we have eyes illumined by faith, we can look on this divine array the way our Christian forebears have done for centuries: With faith's insight, we know that God set these sparkling gems against the black velvet of night to delight each of us, his beloved children, and to show us his splendid might and mystery.

You, with the eyes of a Christian parent, can perceive even deeper meaning. As you sweep your gaze across the heavens, let your mind thrill with this wondrous idea: Countless ages ago, before those stars took fire, God placed you—you, personally, by name—within his eternal plan. It was then that he called you to your divine life's mission.

God knew then, and knows now, everything about you: all the great and small events of your life, your childhood and upbringing, your gifts and flaws and sins, the destiny of your whole life throughout this slip of human history in which he placed you. He knew all those souls whose lives intertwine with your own, including your parents and friends, spouse and children, from the moment of your conception to the appointed hour of your passage to eternity.

11

St. James wondered at this mystery with these words to the early Christians: ". . . what is your life? For you are a mist that appears for a little time and then vanishes" (4:14). Every life, though brief and fleeting, has a destined part in God's eternal will.

And you? From all eternity, he called you personally, by your name, to serve him by serving those closest to you, starting with your family. He sent you your children, one by one, gave each of them a destiny woven through your own, and he beseeches you to lead their souls back to him.

He, the all-powerful Creator, needs you—counts on your free dedication, your generous consent to his will—to form in your children a truthful conscience, to strengthen their minds and wills, to enkindle in their hearts a lifelong love for him and ambitions for a life of holy, sacrificial service. He asks you to surpass yourself, expend yourself in joyful self-giving, to guide your children to become, with his never-failing help, great men and women—saints in the middle of the world.

To direct the destiny of your children's souls, their earthly and eternal happiness, is your sacred mission. This is God's will for you from all eternity, your great vocation as a parent.

If you wish to know God's will for you as a father or mother, you should begin with God's promises to you in his holy Scriptures. In the lines inspired by the Holy Spirit, you can trace the lineaments of your mission. From his divine word, you can draw out the hope and strength you need to carry out God's eternal will for your family.

Read what God said through Jeremiah to describe the dazzling essence of a divine vocation, including your own. The Holy Spirit, the Spirit of Love, directs these words of promise to you:

> For I know the plans I have for you, says the LORD, plans for welfare and not for evil, to give you a future and a hope. Then you will call upon me and come and pray to me, and I

will hear you. You will seek me and find me; when you seek me with all your heart, I will be found by you, says the LORD, and I will restore your fortunes . . . (Jer 29:11–14).

If you are like other Christian mothers and fathers, you have experienced from time to time a precious and beautiful moment in family life, an occasion when the full meaning of your holy vocation wells up within you and tugs at your heart, and that poignant moment is this: You tiptoe into your child's bedroom at night and peer down at your little one lying peacefully in sleep.

For Christian parents, this is almost a religious experience. You look down at your little child with the tenderest affection and a kind of breath-catching awe. You sense the nearness of God there with you, for your child is a living miracle—a priceless gift bestowed on you by the Author of Life.

As you see your child's little chest rise and fall gently with the breath of life, you sense yourself in the presence of mystery, and your mind turns in wonder to things of the spirit: the mystery of the gift of life, the creation of an eternal soul, the playing out of a destiny until the moment of death, the adventures and dangers that lie in the years ahead, and your awesome responsibility to lead this little one to a great life—and then home to God.

At this precious moment, or whenever you turn to reflect on your divine calling as a parent, direct your thoughts to these words of the Holy Spirit spoken through the prophet Isaiah (55:8–9):

> For my thoughts are not your thoughts,
>   neither are your ways my ways, says the LORD.
> For as the heavens are higher than the earth,
>   so are my ways higher than your ways
>   and my thoughts than your thoughts.

Be confident that God has far-reaching plans for you and

13

your spouse and each of your children, plans far beyond the reach of your highest imaginings.

God's appointed destiny for you, your family's life-adventure, will come to pass if you seek to know his will, strive to embrace it, and take courage from his promises and his all-powerful help.

Bear this hopeful vision always in your heart: You and your family have been called to do great things now and in the years to come, to play your part in God's designs to renew the face of the earth.

Every vocation calls for some sort of leadership.

Fathers and mothers—all types of men and women with different gifts and flaws and temperaments—surpass their limitations and win out in family life through confident leadership. Christian parents base that confidence on knowing they have a sacred mission to carry out with their children. They see themselves rearing adults, not children.

Conscientious Christian parents, like you, know they have been called by God to carry out a holy task: to lead their children, with daily sacrificial effort, to grow into confident, responsible, generous men and women who are committed to live by Christian principles all their lives, no matter what the cost.

Being conscious of this sacred mission, holding it always before their eyes, is what turns parents into great men and women themselves, real heroes to their children, and makes their family life together a beautiful adventure.

It has been said that any hard work bereft of some high ideal settles like sludge into dreary, pointless drudgery; but that same work, driven and shaped by a great love, turns normal life into noble adventure.

This is vitally important to understand: When God sends you a child, he calls you to an adventure.

He whispers a promise to you: "This child has received the gift of life from a great love, both yours and mine. I call you to work as my holy instrument to lead this little one, day by day, one small step at a time, to become the masterpiece I had in mind from all eternity. If you join your will with mine—if you let me into *your* life—I will act *through* you to make this child strong and holy, and I will pour out on your family the blessed joys of earthly and eternal life. So, trust in me; have confidence in my promise. All I ask is that you do the best you can. Struggle to surpass yourself in loving service, and leave the rest to my almighty power...."

Every divine vocation is a call to service.

When we receive the waters of Baptism and are called to a new life, each of us receives a mission from God to serve him by serving others—to let God, as it were, use us as his instruments for the earthly and eternal happiness of others.

This holy service—like any excellent service in everyday affairs—calls for humility, an eye for the bodily and spiritual needs of others, generous self-sacrifice, and patient effort, including the effort of patient teaching.

One of the most striking scenes in the Gospel of St. John is that in which Jesus, in the midst of the Last Supper and nearing the climax of his redemptive mission, lays aside his garments, girds himself with a towel, prepares a water vessel, and washes the feet of his disciples (13: 1–17).

To people of the Middle East at that time, who walked everywhere in sandals through dust, one's feet, nearly always caked in sweat and dirt, were considered an ignoble part of the body. So the task of washing another's feet was a humiliation, something to be done only by the lowest class of servants. John the Baptist alluded to the lowliness of this task when he said of Jesus the Messiah: "After me comes he who is mightier than I, the thong of whose sandals I am not worthy to stoop down and untie" (Mk 1: 7).

So Christ stooped down and humbled himself, and this he did to dramatize a vital point. He said plainly, "... I have given you an example, that you also should do as I have done to

15

you. . . . If you know these things, blessed are you if you do them."

The lesson? Each of us, his followers, is called to generous, self-denying service. And parents, ever aware of their special call, should imitate Christ's example in their family affairs: serving their family and all others in their lives, setting aside the wiles of pride, status, comfort, and convenience. To serve this way is to pray. To serve this way is to become like Christ himself.

Your mission as a parent is to lead your children to *see the invisible*.

As you know from your family life, children have highly selective hearing, but their roving, agile little eyes miss nothing. What your children witness in your life and hear from your lips should lead them, day by day in your years together, to set in their minds and hearts those invisible realities that shape our faith and make for a great, saintly life: *God, the soul, life of grace, the reality of sin, conscience, hope, charity, honesty, honor, integrity, the presence of Christ in his Church, the life-giving power of sacramental confession, the presence of God within us and around us and above all in the Sacred Host.*

If you neglect to teach the invisible, as so many parents do, your children could grow up to live as materialists.

Young people who learn nothing about life's spiritual dimension will enmesh themselves in the material: pleasure, power, sex, the constant yearning for money and possessions. Their lives will center wholly on themselves and their senses, their egos and their things. They will be driven to live like beasts, or technically skilled barbarians. They'll never progress from serving self to serving others, and their hope-deprived lives—like those of so many people today—will ricochet frantically, pointlessly, between pleasure and despair.

What is this materialistic life-outlook? How can you better understand it so you can warn your children to shun it all their lives? Look at it from this perspective...

Materialism does not mean, as many suppose, merely the avid pursuit of things—fashionable clothes and cars, trendy or expensive gadgets, a hefty portfolio. This consumerist lust is only part of the problem. For, after all, many people, even the well-to-do, can possess all sorts of things without living as materialists.

Materialism really means *seeing and treating other people as things*. Materialism considers man (in the philosophical sense) as a mere object, a clever beast. This is where the evil lies.

This twisted life-outlook directly affects the way people see life and treat other human beings. It has several bedrock premises:

- Life ends with death; so there's no reward or punishment in any afterlife.
- We answer to no Higher Power for the way we live; we answer only to the law, if it can catch us.
- We can do anything we want to anyone, as long as it's legal.
- Conscience is nothing but a tangle of sentiments, a residue of childhood naïveté.
- Morality is merely social convention.
- "Rights" are really disguised interests and rationalized power-grabbing.
- Because human beings are objects, whatever things we want—money, possessions, fame, power—can come ahead of people.
- Work is for money, and money is for power and a pleasure-glutted life.
- The only real evil is pain.
- Life has no purpose but the pursuit of pleasure and power.

This heartless and godless outlook on life—the dogma that man is only a beast—is the antithesis of Christian morality, indeed of basic decency among people of good will. Yet we find

17

it promoted aggressively in business and professional affairs, trumpeted in the media and in public life. Indeed, we find it, as we look all around us, seeping its way like acid into family life.

So your vocation is to lead your children, by your own splendid life, to shun materialism and live like another Christ. You are called by God to show your children the beauty and power of spiritual life, the great reality of what's invisible.

A mission, any mission, calls for some sort of job description. As we might expect, the job designed by God for Catholic parents is, like his Sacred Scriptures, a blending of both the practical and the sublime.

Broadly speaking, parents take on the task of leading their children to set within their souls the seven great virtues of Christian living. This they do in three ways: through their personal example, their leadership in making children do the right thing repeatedly until it sets as a habit (that is, directed practice), and their verbal explanation of right and wrong.

Savvy parents know that their children are forming habits every single day; the question is, which ones? Good habits, those actions and attitudes practiced every day, turn eventually into virtues. As poet John Dryden put it, "We first make our habits. Then our habits make us."

So, what are these seven great virtues that Christian parents set out to teach their children for life?

Faith. Because we trust Jesus Christ (who said "Trust me" in so many ways), we believe all that he taught us about himself, his redemptive mission, his "kingdom without end" (the Church), our earthly mission as his followers, our eternal destiny in his friendship. The word *Catholic* means "all"—and we see this "all-ness" of our Faith in Matthew 28:19–20: "*All* authority in heaven and on earth has been given to me. Go therefore and make disciples of *all* nations, baptizing them in the name of the Father and of the Son and of the Holy Spirit, teaching them to observe *all* that I have commanded you; and behold, I am with you always, until the close of the age."

Hope. We trust God to grant us the means for our salvation, and we trust in his loving Providence. Therefore, no problem on earth is insurmountable, and indeed, as St. Paul told us, "We know that in everything God works for good with those who love him" (Rom 8:28).

Charity. We love God above all things and we love all people as our brothers and sisters. Love, real love, is not sweet sentiments; it is the willingness and power to endure hardships, problems, tedium, and disappointment for the sake of others' welfare and happiness. Like all other great loves on earth, love for God and his Church means sacrifice. When we seek to become like Christ, then our daily acts of sacrifice join with his for the redemption of mankind.

Prudence (sound judgment). This is the ability to assess the important distinctions in life, the acquired power to discern truth from falsehood, good from evil, the noble from the squalid. It is an active, healthy interest in people, current affairs, and culture (that is, a cordial familiarity with the finest achievements of the human spirit), all given vigor by serious study. On the moral plane, sound judgment means a well formed conscience, the voice of our parents.

Justice (sense of responsibility). This vital virtue means giving God and others what is due to them; it means putting duty ahead of comfort, self-interest, and self-centered "feelings." Parents should teach their children this: The only feelings that really count in our home are those springing from our love for God and each other; all other feelings take second place to our duties of love. Responsibility means carrying out our duties so that others won't suffer; hence responsibility is a form of love. We are put here on earth to serve God and each other.

Fortitude (courageous perseverance, personal toughness, "guts"). This is the power to endure or overcome hardship, pain, disappointments, setbacks, anxiety, tedium. It also means the strength to appear a bit "different" from our contemporaries, for the Christian life makes us, as always in history, "different."

Temperance (self-mastery, self-control). Self-mastery is the power to enjoy the good things of life in moderation. It means having enough inner strength to overcome the allurements of self-interest and self-indulgence. It means being able to wait for things, practicing good manners, letting our courtesy show others our respect for their rights and dignity and sensibilities. Temperance is, in a word, "class."

What should drive you on in your vocation, steel you to persevere through anything, is the utter importance of your leading your children to a lifelong friendship with God. This mission, calling for years of prayer and patient perseverance, is literally a matter of life and death.

For your children's sake, and for your own, please bear this awesome fact in the forefront of your thoughts: It is hell itself—what St. John called the "second death"—that threatens your children.

Hell exists. Hell is real. Many times in Scripture, God, who is all truth, warned us about this horrific reality. Listen to his words:

"Whoever causes one of these little ones who believe in me to sin, it would be better for him if a great millstone were hung round his neck and he were thrown into the sea. And if your hand causes you to sin, cut it off; it is better for you to enter life maimed than with two hands to go to hell, to the unquenchable fire. And if your foot causes you to sin, cut it off; it is better for you to enter life lame than with two feet to be thrown into hell. And if your eye causes you to sin, pluck it out; it is better for you to enter the kingdom of God with one than with two eyes to be thrown into hell, where the worm does not die, and the fire is not quenched" (Mk 9:42–48).

"And do not fear those who kill the body but cannot kill the soul; rather fear him who can destroy both soul and body in hell" (Mt 10:28).

"For what will it profit a man, if he gains the whole world and forfeits his life? Or what shall a man give in return for his life?" (Mt 16:26).

"Even now the axe is laid to the root of the trees; every tree therefore that does not bear good fruit is cut down and thrown into the fire. I baptize you with water for repentance, but he who is coming after me is mightier than I, whose sandals I am not worthy to carry; he will baptize you with the Holy Spirit and with fire. His winnowing fork is in his hand, and he will clear his threshing floor and gather his wheat into the granary, but the chaff he will burn with unquenchable fire" (Mt 3: 10–12).

"I tell you, many will come from east and west and sit at table with Abraham, Isaac, and Jacob in the kingdom of heaven, while the sons of the kingdom will be thrown into the outer darkness; there men will weep and gnash their teeth" (Mt 8: 11–12).

"And whoever says a word against the Son of man will be forgiven; but whoever speaks against the Holy Spirit will not be forgiven, either in this age or in the age to come" (Mt 12: 32–33).

"Then the king said to the attendants, 'Bind him hand and foot, and cast him into the outer darkness; there men will weep and gnash their teeth.' For many are called, but few are chosen" (Mt 22: 13–14).

"Before him will be gathered all the nations, and he will separate them one from another as a shepherd separates the sheep from the goats, and he will place the sheep at his right hand, but the goats at the left. . . . Then he will say to those at his left hand, 'Depart from me, you cursed, into the eternal fire prepared for the devil and his angels.' . . . And they will go away into eternal punishment, but the righteous into eternal life." (Mt 25: 32–33, 41, 46)

"Truly I say to you, all sins will be forgiven the sons of men, and whatever blasphemies they utter; but whoever blasphemes against the Holy Spirit never has forgiveness, but is guilty of an eternal sin" (Mk 3: 28–29).

"Even now the axe is laid to the root of the trees; every tree therefore that does not bear good fruit is cut down and thrown into the fire. . . . He will baptize you with the Holy Spirit and with fire. His winnowing fork is in his hand, to clear his threshing floor, and to gather the wheat into his granary, but the chaff he will burn with unquenchable fire" (Lk 3: 9, 16–17).

"The rich man also died and was buried; and in Hades, being in torment, he lifted up his eyes, and saw Abraham far off and Lazarus in his bosom. And he called out, 'Father Abraham, have mercy upon me, and send Lazarus to dip the end of his finger in water and cool my tongue; for I am in anguish in this flame.'" (Lk 16:22–24).

"He who believes in the Son has eternal life; he who does not obey the Son shall not see life, but the wrath of God rests upon him" (Jn 3:36).

"He who conquers shall not be hurt by the second death" (Rev 2:11).

"See that you do not despise one of these little ones, for I tell you that in heaven their angels always behold the face of my Father who is in heaven. . . . So it is not the will of my Father who is in heaven that one of these little ones should perish" (Mt 18:10, 14).

What is the motivating ideal of your vocation as a parent? What sort of men and women should your children, with God's help, grow to be? What should their lives look like by the time they reach the full flower of adulthood, before they're even out of their teens?

See how the prophet Micah expressed the ideal for living a great life: "He has showed you, O man, what is good; and what does the Lord require of you but to do justice, and to love kindness, and to walk humbly with your God?" (6:8).

If your children live this way—if they do right, love kindness, and walk in truth with God—then they will grow up, with God's grace, to become men and women with the same dispositions.

All their lives, they will cherish in their hearts a love for Jesus Christ and his Church. Unlike the crowds around them, they will not envision God as a shapeless abstraction, nor his Church as a merely human "structure," nor his doctrine as a dreary set of propositions, nor his will as a list of threatening rules. On the contrary, your children will know and love God

for the gifts of life, see his
rve others as he does, and
m.

r conscience: strong, clear,
nce will be the memory of
t will be the voice of God
e remembered words and

. They will have excellent,
ents, and ideas; a will that
tude so firm that they can
e; and the delight of enjoy-
nd great blessings that he
ay, peace, prosperity, and
nts of modern life. Fully
e, living examples of what
ves glory to God as much

n charity with everyone.
s does, with compassion-
orgiveness. They will be
de the shade of past inju-
endship.
le service, directing their
good of others. They will
, a call for us to surpass
ourselves, a sacrifice we undertake so that others will not suffer.

Though deeply pious, they will not shrink back from the world in fear and loathing, nor will they live as oddballs. On the contrary, they will love the world as God gave it to us, as Christ embraced it, as our home—the *mise-en-scène* for acting out the epic drama of our salvation.

They will live as upright citizens: well informed, maturely discerning, generously active in civic affairs. They will collaborate with friends to turn around those evils that Mohandas Gandhi, the liberator of India, rightly called the "seven social sins"—namely, politics without principle, pleasure without conscience, wealth without work, education without character, business without morality, science without humanity, and worship without sacrifice.

All their lives, they will retain the same great loves they had as children: love for God, love for family, love for life itself, and love for the truth. They will shine forth with all the powers of competent, responsible adults illuminated with the hearts of children. They will become what Christ called all of us to be, "wise as serpents, and innocent as doves."

All of this is a noble ideal. But not impossible. Remember, children strongly tend to grow *up* to our expectations—or *down* to them.

Experienced Christian parents can tell you this: If you try only to *control* your children, you will meet with endless hassles and frustration. You will entangle yourself in vexations and multiply your mistakes. But if you try to *form* your children—to empower their consciences, minds, and wills for life—you will have, with God's help, not merely a fighting chance to succeed but a *fighting certainty*. In the end, your mistakes along the way will not matter. As your children grow, you will know the inner peace of striving to do the best you can; and then, once they've grown, the joy and peace of final triumph.

When this ideal for their children's grown-up life is set before them, many fathers and mothers feel out of their depth, almost completely overwhelmed.

Understandably so. Their small children are so often relentlessly active, blithely self-centered and cunning, resistant to direction, unreasonable and irrational, and, so much of the time, nearly out of control. The challenging task of forming them into strong and saintly grown-ups can seem daunting, at times even impossible.

If you, like many other parents, feel the burden of your task, bear some lessons in mind from the history of salvation.

In Sacred Scripture, we see one fact recur: Every time God

sends someone a mission for the welfare of others, he sets it as a seemingly "insoluble" problem. A vocation from God means hefting upon our shoulders some unreasonable burden, being confronted with an apparently impossible obstacle. Consider these examples.

As an old man, long past the power of fatherhood, Abraham was called by God to be the father and founder of a great nation, and he was directed, as a test of his faith, to slay his beloved son, Isaac. We know what happened. Abraham's trust in God laid the foundation in history for our salvation. And through his example of loving trust shines forth God's promise to parents: "Love me, trust me, no matter what, and I will save your children. Do not be afraid. . . ."

The patriarch Joseph, betrayed by his brothers and sold into slavery, was thereby set up by God's providence to save his people later in time of famine. The lesson? *God knows what he is doing.* God can use even tragic betrayal and wickedness to work his will for our salvation—as he did again on Calvary.

Moses was called to contend with the mightiest political forces of his time, to redeem his people from bondage, lead them through a hostile wilderness, withstand their ingratitude and rebellion, and save them.

David, an adolescent, wholly without military experience and resources, was called by God to lead an armed host and free his people from their enemies on all sides.

Mary of Nazareth was called to be both virgin and mother, an "impossible" situation, and thus become the mother of all Christians till the end of time.

Then, after Christ won our Redemption, we see this same dynamic in Church history, the triumph of sanctity over impossible problems.

The Apostles, reckoned by their enemies as "ignorant nobodies," worked miracles in Christ's name and evangelized the whole world.

Down the centuries, holy missionaries answered the call of God to evangelize masses of people enslaved to vice, idolatry, ignorance of God and human destiny—including our own heathen ancestors. With God's help and through their sacrifices, these bearers of God's good news persevered and succeeded. They baptized and won the hearts of our forebears, and so we now hold their Faith as our legacy, that treasure of good news handed forward from parents to children through the centuries, and now to us.

God calls you too as a missionary to your children. For the Church has seen one truth about family life recur in history: *every generation of children must be missionized.* If not, they are lost to the aggressive, relentlessly encroaching forces of evil, what St. Paul called "the dominion of darkness"—and their family line plunges once again into godlessness, unrestrained pleasure-pursuit, and despair.

Like Paul and Francis Xavier and Isaac Jogues, you are called to evangelization. You are summoned to civilize and missionize those beloved, active little "heathens" tearing around your house. Your heavenly Father counts on you to embrace this call.

So don't be afraid. With God's help, you will win your children's hearts and souls.

Remember what God spoke to Mary through the angel Gabriel when he announced her vocation: "For with God nothing will be impossible" (Lk 1:37).

Your vocation calls for leadership. How can we understand confident leadership? Look at it this way . . .

Confident parents are effective leaders with their children. In fact, this confidence, all by itself, nearly always makes up for parents' shortcomings and blunders along the way.

In the normal course of human affairs, what leads some people to be confident and to raise confident children? Aside from inborn temperament, we can observe these things:

- Confident people grow up in a family surrounded by love.
- Confident people have a habit, built through years of prac-

tice, of attacking and solving problems, usually with success. So, in the face of adversity, they know they have at least a fighting chance. Courage, as the saying goes, is the memory of past successes.

- They undertake a mission so vitally important that it brings out the best in them.
- They know that someplace on this earth they enjoy the support of one or more loved ones who are absolutely crazy about them.

These generalizations hold true for most confident parents, even those with little faith. But those parents who put their trust in God have even better reasons to be confident. . . .

God's almighty help is ours for the asking, every time. So, with his help, we are always empowered to make a fresh start in life. The Gospels and the history of the Church are filled with tales of troubled people, even from dysfunctional families, who begin life anew, become great men and women, transform themselves into saints. A man or woman who trusts in God need not be a victim of the past, no matter how troubled or lamentable it may have been. Christ, who overcame sin and death, can overcome anything that entangles our lives.

Christ said, "Learn from me, for I am meek and humble of heart."

We are meek when we hear his word, embrace his will, and live by it. We are humble when we trust him to bridge that dark chasm which often yawns before us in dealing with our children—that gap between the outermost edge of our limitations and the task ahead of us, the distance between the very best we can do and what remains to be done. When we ask God's help, his power spans the distance, enlarges our grasp. As he promised, he brings our efforts to completion.

We need not waste time trying to change ourselves all by ourselves, a daunting and impossible task. Our Lord came among us not only to save us from hell, but also to straighten out our lives, *to cure the absence of God in our lives.* He said, "I am the way, the truth, and the life." So if we let him inside

27

us—if we become one with his mind, and will, and heart, and mission—it is he who will change us. It is he, working through us, who will work subtle miracles in our family life and bring our children to truth and life and salvation.

God calls you to be a leader to your children—but remember, a leader has joiners, not followers. In other words, you are called to live like a saint—a child of God, committed to a life of loving service in his name—and to lead your children to *join* you in living this way.

You will do this mostly by your example. Jesus' name means "Savior," and so you should appear to your children—with your radiant, grateful gladness and constant charity, the approach to life of one who has been saved.

You will lead also by prompting your children to join you in acts of piety and service. You will respect your children's freedom, the freedom that is God's greatest gift to each of us, and teach them to use it responsibly, that is, with a spirit of service to others and to God. Someone once summed up the mission of parents like this: *to walk the children through the giving of self.*

And you will lead them by your words of instruction, correction, and encouragement, as Jesus did with his disciples.

Example, directed practice, and word—these, with reliance on God's unfailing help, are the ways you will shape your children, through years of prayerful perseverance, into valiant, saintly men and women

As you go about forming your children, recall this insightful adage of teaching:

What children only hear, they mostly forget.
What they see, they mostly remember.
What they do, they understand and internalize for life.

If you dedicate yourself to teaching holiness and virtue to your children, you will know the blessed reward God promised to teachers in the book of Daniel (12:3): "And those who are wise shall shine like the brightness of the firmament; and those who turn many to righteousness, like the stars for ever and ever."

In 1985, Pope John Paul II laid out the Church's most pressing need for our time. His words express the essence of your God-bestowed mission with your children. This is what he said:

> There is a need for heralds of the Gospel who are experts in humanity, who have a profound knowledge of the heart of present-day man, participating in his joys and hopes, in his anguish and his sadness, and who are at the same time contemplatives in love with God. For this we need new saints. . . . We must beseech the Lord to increase the Church's spirit of holiness and send us new saints to evangelize today's world.

Heralds of the Gospel . . . experts in humanity . . . contemplatives in love with God . . . new saints to evangelize today's world. With the help of God and his Blessed Mother, and your holy sacrifices as a parent, this is what your family will present to the Church and to the world.

2.

Face to Face with Jesus Christ

Your sacred mission, the vital core of your vocation, is to light a fire of love for God in the heart of each of your children.

A love for Jesus and his Church, formed from infancy, will direct the whole course of your children's lives—and save them. To succeed at this mission, with God's never-failing help, is to succeed in everything.

In his encyclical *Faith and Reason*, Pope John Paul II spoke about how the virtues of faith, hope, and love are interrelated, or different facets of the same jewel, different approaches to the same central truth.

Faith is not, as some would say, a leap in the dark. Rather, it is our acceptance of what is revealed to us by someone we love and therefore trust. When we love, we trust; when our heart extends to another, we believe.

Our holy Faith has spread through the centuries from heart to heart, parents to children through each generation—like the flames of candles passed from hand to hand in our Easter Vigil liturgy—all set aflame in the beginning with the love exchanged between Christ and his disciples in the early Church.

What does this mean for you and your children? Something vitally important: Your children's life of faith—their acceptance of God's teaching, their embracing of his will—must come from their personal love for Jesus Christ.

Your children's souls will be saved, transported to holiness, not by merely memorizing catechetical points or grasping "what the Church commands" or fearing "what the Church forbids." Along the twisting pathways of their lives, your children will live rightly if you lead them now, in childhood, to love Jesus Christ as a person, as their greatest Friend. They will shun sin, and make amends for it in sacramental confession, if you teach them now, in childhood, to see sin as an offense to Jesus, a hurtful thing calling for heartfelt apology.

Your children will become valiant Christian men and women if you lead them by your example and words to see the face of Jesus—and how Jesus looks at them with heartfelt affection in every moment of every day.

To introduce your children to Jesus Christ, to describe him in all the richness and grace of his splendid personality, you must read the Gospels. You must read the evangelists slowly, thoughtfully, prayerfully. When you know and befriend Jesus through the Gospels, you can lead your children to picture him, hear him, see his face.

This is what Christ asks of you. In the Gospels, Jesus calls himself "Son of man" more than eighty times—as if to insist that he is one of us, has come to dwell among us because he loves us, and wants us to love him back. Look your youngsters in the eye and teach them this: Our religion is not a set of practices; it is, above all else, a love affair.

Whatever you teach your children about Jesus and how he looks at each of them—whatever you do to make the Gospels come alive in their minds and hearts—will remain within them, bolster them to resist temptation, anchor their hope through the storms of life that await them.

What we learn about Jesus in childhood has lifelong consequences. A love affair set afire in the pure heart of a child remains within, unblemished, through the course of life.

Take comfort from a remarkable passage recounted by Eusebius, one of the great early Church writers (*Historia Ecclesiae* 5.20, 5–7). The words are taken from a letter written by Irenaeus, Bishop of Lyons, in the second century. This saint fondly recalls how he learned his faith as a boy from listening to St. Polycarp, an early Church martyr who was a disciple of St. John the Evangelist. This is his memory:

> I remember the events of those days more clearly than those which happened recently, for what we learn as children grows up with the soul and is united to it, so that I can speak even of the place in which the blessed Polycarp sat and disputed, how he came in and went out, the character of his life, the appearance of his body, the discourses which he made to the people, how he reported his friendship with John and with the others who had seen the Lord, how he remembered their words, and what were the things concerning the Lord which he had heard from them, and about their miracles, and about their teachings, and how Polycarp had received them from the eyewitnesses of the Word of Life, and reported all things in agreement with the Scriptures. I listened eagerly even then to these things through the mercy of God which was given me and made notes of them, not on paper, but in my heart, and ever by the grace of God do I truly ruminate on them.

In one of his beautiful, prophetic passages, Isaiah said, "A little child shall lead them" (11:6) These words, inspired by the Holy Spirit, the Spirit of Love, carry special meaning for you as a parent. They hint at the power of spiritual childhood.

How can you summon to life within your soul an intimate, heart-to-heart relationship with God, a fervent friendship that will direct the course of your life and the lives of your children? The answer is spiritual childhood.

Set yourself to live as a beloved child of your heavenly father, always alive to his presence, always trusting in his help, always eager to do his will and please him.

You can shape a clearer picture of how to live this way by calling to mind those special times in family life when you sense a special welling up of love for your children, when you feel your heart moved with tender affection for them. You know what these moments are:

When your small children, absorbed in play, pause to glance up and smile at you, just because you're there beside them.

When they wrap their little arms around your neck and fall asleep on your shoulder, trusting in your powerful protection.

When they're afraid of the dark or some crashing thunderstorm and crawl into bed beside you.

When, all upset and on the verge of tears, they climb up onto your lap and spill out some "big problem" that weighs on them.

When they're sorry they did wrong and plead with tears for your forgiveness.

When they do the right thing without being told, just to please you.

When they show kindness and forgiveness toward their brothers and sisters.

When they surprise you with a gift they fashioned for you with their hands—a scrawled picture, a clay figure, a little bunch of flowers—to show their love for you, to return the love you have for them.

When they share laughter with you, the sheer delight in being alive and safe.

When they close their eyes in prayer to Jesus and Mary.

When you tiptoe into their bedrooms at night and look down on them sleeping.

The lesson? Learn from your children how to trust God, how to offer him your work and joys and sorrows, how to love him—as your children love you—with all your heart and soul and mind and strength.

And from your own tender love for each of your children, learn how God looks at you and loves you passionately, his dearly beloved child.

Jesus Christ became man not only to save us from the "second death" but also, in his words, that we "may have life, and have

34

it more abundantly." Christ came to *cure the absence of God in people's lives.*

Jesus lives forever as our Savior, and we Christians are therefore conscious of being saved—not only from hell, but also from a life blind to the presence of God, a life lived in darkness.

Religion, it is said, is an acute awareness of the presence and power of God, and of his love for each person. A Christian is acutely aware of these things. He is conscious of being saved, and therefore he is happy; his life is marked by gratitude and a desire to serve others.

So when we speak of sanctifying "ordinary" life, what do we mean? How can we understand a holiness that suffuses, enlivens, and gives light to everyday affairs?

Consider it this way . . .

The pages of the Gospels show how Jesus, the Christ, with a mere turning of his will, cured crowds of wretched people from their dread afflictions: blindness, deafness, paralysis, leprosy, and diabolic possession.

Use your imagination to fill out this picture: What happened to each of these people after they were saved? How were their lives changed?

For the real gift Jesus gave to them and their families was what they had most longed for, *normal life.* Each of these men and women could now work, form a family, live the same daily life as everyone else around them. But with a great difference!

Conscious of being saved, they felt moved with heartfelt gratitude to God every day for the rest of their lives. From the moment they were cured, they saw all the commonplace things of daily life—family, friends, sight, hearing, work, play, health, education, peace of mind—as wonderful gifts from God.

They could hold a job as others did; no more begging. So they found joy in their work, delight in turning their newfound powers to the service of others.

They were profoundly and joyfully apostolic. Their transcendent gratitude led them to intimate love for Jesus Christ, their savior. They would speak of Jesus warmly and

35

enthusiastically to anyone whose lives crossed their own, and would wish to share with everyone their deep happiness, the "good news" of Christ's love and salvation.

So what does it mean to sanctify everyday life? It means to think and live like those people after they were saved, after they received the precious gift of normal life. It means to be moved by gratitude throughout every day and to share this joy with others.

The apostle Paul wrote many exhortations to his children in the Faith, nearly all of whom were parents like you. In one of his letters to the Thessalonians, he summed up the way all of us should live as Christians: "Rejoice always, pray constantly, give thanks in all circumstances; for this is the will of God in Christ Jesus for you. Do not quench the Spirit" (1 Thess 5: 16–19).

This is counsel to remember and live by in your busy family life: Always be happy. Never stop praying. Give thanks to God for everything, even those problems, large or small, that may tempt your patience and hope. Do not snuff out those promptings of the Holy Spirit enkindled within you. Open your eyes to God's blessings in your daily affairs, see him in your children's souls, and set aside some time each day to converse with him, heart to heart, in prayer.

In the fourth century, St. Jerome offered words of advice to a mother eager to improve her spiritual life. His holy counsel to that good woman still imparts wisdom to any Christian parent. This is what he said:

> Look after the upkeep of your home in such a way that you also give some repose to your soul. Choose an appropriate place, a little apart from the family din, and take refuge

there as in a harbor, as one who escapes a great storm of worries. Quiet down, with the tranquility of your retreat, the waves of concerns stirred up by external affairs. Put such effort and fervor into reading Sacred Scripture, let your prayers follow so closely one upon another, make thought of the future life so steady and constant, that you abundantly offset with your repose all the preoccupations of your remaining hours. I do not say this to try to keep you from your loved ones; rather, I am trying to help you learn to meditate on how you should behave toward them" (*Letter* 148, no. 24).

The natural leaning of youngsters and adolescents is to imitate people they admire. Unconsciously they adopt whatever attitudes they perceive in their heroes. This is how they shape their deepest values—what matters most to them, the compass that directs their moral choices—and indeed their whole outlook on life.

If parents win out as heroic leaders to their sons and daughters, then their children will absorb their life-outlook and values.

Spiritual directors have long noticed this phenomenon. From time to time they encounter young people who take their Faith seriously, turn to God in prayer, live a sacramental life, commit themselves to chastity, have eyes for the needs of others. Excellent, admirable young adults.

And what do these young people have in common? Again and again the same pattern appears. Each of them had at least one parent who lived this way—took the Faith seriously, prayed to God confidently, attended Mass during the week, made frequent confession, even sacrificed to make an annual retreat.

The power of example. Remember that your children are always watching you. They look, they assess, and they remember. You do the most good for them when you're scarcely aware of it.

If you can possibly manage it, make an annual retreat. Do whatever is necessary to take a weekend out of your busy life and devote it to prayer, give it wholly to God.

Reflect on these words from the prophet Isaiah: "For thus said the Lord GOD, the Holy One of Israel, 'In returning and rest you shall be saved; in quietness and in trust shall be your strength'" (30:15).

This is what a retreat gives to us: "Returning and rest, ... quietness and trust, ... strength." This is why so many busy fathers and mothers *make* the time for a retreat.

A lot happens to them in these days of prayer and reflection.

They pull themselves away, if only for a couple of days, from the rush and tangle of their busy lives—the phone calls, deadlines, scheduled appointments, and countless tasks that tug at their attention. They set aside whatever is seemingly "urgent" and enjoy some much-needed physical rest: peace and quiet wholly apart from their normal lives.

From this distance, they gain a realistic perspective on their lives—present, past, and future. They see their life as God sees it and thereby recast their priorities. They see what's really important in their lives and what's not. They see new avenues for personal growth in family and work. They see, often for the first time, God's loving providential hand in their lives so far, and his holy will for them now and in the years to come. Their lives make more sense.

They draw near to the heart of Christ through prayer, reading, reflection, the Eucharist, and the sacrament of reconciliation. For the first time since childhood, they express their love for God simply and ardently, and they grow to trust entirely in his promise, "Ask and you shall receive . . ." They grow in confidence.

Through confession and personal spiritual direction, they set aside any burdens of the past that weighed them down, troubled their peace of mind—anxieties, personal conflicts, unresolved problems, buried-away but unforgotten tangles of conscience. With God's help, they resolve these and find peace. They return from the retreat with the light heart and the clear conscience they knew in childhood, the potent joy of being alive and in the state of grace.

They give excellent, life-directing example to their children.

Eddie Cantor, the Broadway entertainer, once said, "It takes twenty years to produce an overnight hit." To be a great parent, you need patience, often an abundance of patience. And patience, let us never forget, is a virtue. Patience is a habit built up over time into a power—and it is, moreover, a gift of the Holy Spirit.

Learn from Jesus' example how to be patient with your family, and also with yourself.

What patience Jesus had with his disciples! For three years he endured their flaws and backsliding and blindness to his teaching. Though his Apostles heard his words and witnessed his miracles, and even worked miracles themselves, they showed a rocklike resistance to change. They flamed in anger with each other, pushed for first place, argued which of them was the greatest. They mistook their Master's meaning, shrank in terror from adversity (as during the storm on the lake), fell asleep while he suffered in Gethsemane, and ran away as cowards in his hour of greatest need.

All in all, they were vain, quarrelsome, thick-headed, narrowly impelled to personal advantage. Spoiled children. Yet Jesus loved them, had plans for them, changed them utterly with his grace.

For, with all their faults, his disciples had inner strengths that Jesus could build on.

Though so often they failed to grasp his teaching, they trusted him. Though their minds were clouded by ego and ignorance, their hearts were set on him and his promises. Somehow, they sensed, he would make things turn out all right—though at the time they failed to see how. When Jesus announced his miracle of the Eucharist (John 6), and many mistrustful followers walked away in indignation, Peter and the handful remained. Peter said to Jesus for all of them, "Lord, to whom shall we go? You have the words of eternal life." Peter said to Christ, in effect: We don't understand, but if you say so, it must be true. We put our trust in you.

Aside from trusting Christ, they were humble. That is, at some deep level they recognized the truth about themselves. Even with their vain ambitions, they acknowledged that they were flawed, sinful men. When Jesus announced at his Last Supper that one of them would betray him, each asked in dismay, "Is it I, Lord?" That is, they knew they were capable of any wrong. And this truth—the same that we admit in sincere sacramental confession—is what Jesus took in hand to make them surpass themselves, to turn them into valiant saints.

What can we learn from this? No matter how great our faults and sins, Jesus can lead us by the hand to greatness. If, that is, we have the trust and humility of small children—that power of spiritual childhood which we cultivate through frequent confession.

In all three Synoptic Gospels—Matthew 8–9, Mark 5, and Luke 8—the Holy Spirit recounts four dramatic miracles of Jesus, as if all four together underscored some vital point:

Our Lord is curled up asleep in Peter's boat when a great storm surges to life on the Lake of Genesareth. Wild, shrieking winds toss the boat violently, and great waves crash against its sides. His disciples panic and cry to Jesus for help. He awakes, upbraids them for their lack of faith, and then, to their astonishment, calms the storm.

Later, when stepping ashore at the land of the pagan Gerasenes, Jesus forcibly expels a ferocious legion of demons from a possessed man.

Later still, Jesus extends his healing power to a woman afflicted with a chronic flow of blood, a poor sufferer who had such faith in him that she sought only to touch the edge of his garment.

40

Finally, Jesus hears the desperate pleas of Jairus, a grief-stricken father whose little girl lay on the point of death, and then raises his daughter to life.

What do these four dramatic miracles signify? Simply this: Jesus has absolute power over nature, over the wiles and forces of hell, over bodily illness, and over death itself. What else is there to fear?

In other words, Jesus has power over everything. Everything, that is, but our own free will, our trust in him, the turning of our hearts to him.

So no matter what afflicts us or distresses us, we must never shrink in despair. If we have heartfelt faith in his power and plead for his loving help, he will save us. When prompted by our trusting faith in him, he can do anything.

When Jesus began his public life, what was the very first thing he preached about? Which of his teachings came before the others?

It was not his divinity, nor his redemptive mission, nor his Real Presence in the Eucharist, nor the primacy of Peter in his immortal Church. These truths would come later.

First it was this: "Repent!"

Repentance of sin opens our hearts to receive the truth. So it was with Mary Magdalene, who loved much because she had so much to repent of.

The truth of our sinfulness, once admitted and atoned for, leads to joyful gratitude, an openness to believe, an eagerness to embrace God's will, and a new beginning in life.

Repentance is the first step toward holiness.

The great English writer and apologist G. K. Chesterton was once asked why he became a Catholic. Though normally a man of many words, he did not respond with an elaborately reasoned answer. He said simply, "Because I wanted my sins forgiven."

Sometimes we come across an unfortunate man or woman, homeless and ravaged by some intractable problem, and we're tempted to say within ourselves, perhaps with a mixture of pity and smugness, "There, but for the grace of God, go I."

But how seldom do we think of this situation in reverse—that is, when we read about a saint, or meet one face to face. At such a time, we should be moved to say to ourselves with humility, "There, but for my *resistance* to the grace of God, go I."

Think this through in the presence of God: Where in my life am I resisting the grace of God? What am I holding onto so stubbornly—my pride, my will, my anger, some repeated sin or unrepented tendency—that thwarts God's plan for me and keeps me from becoming a saint?

Robert Hugh Benson, a great English author and a convert, wrote, "There is no happiness in the world comparable to that of the experience known as conversion."

You will make changes in your children when you open yourself to the Holy Spirit, the Spirit of Love, and entreat him to work changes in you. You have a right, as a child of God, to ask him to convert you, to extend his hand and grant you the healing you need to guide your children as he wills.

Pray these fervent lines from the *Veni, Creator*, that beautiful prayer-poem to the Holy Spirit, a treasure of our Church heritage from the ninth century.

> *Lava quod est sordidum,*
> *Riga quod est aridum,*
> *Sana quod est saucium.*
>   *Flecte quod est rigidum,*
>   *Fove quod est frigidum,*
>   *Rege quod est devium.*

Wash what is filthy,
Water what is parched,
Heal what is wounded.
Bend what is rigid,
Warm what is frigid,
Straighten out what is twisted awry.

Hold high ambitions for each of your children. See your efforts in family life, with God's unfailing help, paying off in this way:

When you work to instill the virtues in your children—sound judgment, a sense of responsibility, persevering courage, and temperance—you will build strong character in your children as they grow to adulthood. They will emerge as confident, responsible men and women—competent and respected leaders, wise and learned, savvy and street-smart, tough-minded and thick-skinned, nobody's fool or pushover, living on top of life, enjoying life to its fullest.

And when you work also to build up a life of faith in your children through the gospel, prayer, and sacraments, you open them for the Holy Spirit's living presence in their souls. You will know the joy of seeing the fruits of the Holy Spirit alive in the hearts of your children: charity, joy, peace, patience, kindness, goodness, generosity, gentleness, faithfulness, modesty, self-control, chastity.

Aim high, in other words, to form the kind of valiant, saintly men and women who will influence the Church and our country in the decades to come: young people who have the powers of adults and the spiritual life of childhood, people "wise as serpents, innocent as doves."

In his letter to the Colossians, St. Paul sketched a portrayal of the Christian life, the way Christ's followers should live and treat each other. It is a brief but beautiful description of the Christian family:

Put on then, as God's chosen ones, holy and beloved, compassion, kindness, lowliness, meekness, and patience, forbearing one another and, if one has a complaint against another, forgiving each other; as the Lord has forgiven you, so you also must forgive. And above all these put on love, which binds everything together in perfect harmony. And let the peace of Christ rule in your hearts, to which indeed you were called in the one body. And be thankful (Col 3:12–15).

In practical terms, how do you foster in your children the infused virtues of faith, hope, and love that they received at Baptism? How do you prepare them to receive the indwelling of the Holy Spirit with all his gifts and fruits? How do you form your children in Christian living?

This is the collective experience of Christian parents:

- You take an active, attentive hand in their catechetical instruction. Bear in mind that your children, years from now, will need to pass on the Faith to your grandchildren, and they may need to do this by themselves with little outside support. At that time, they will fall back on the remembrance of your instruction now. You are storing up a memory for them, giving light and example for them to live by later.

- You make prayer a normal, natural part of family life: prayers before meals, in tough situations (illness, upcoming exams, financial problems), and at bedtime (apologizing to God with an act of contrition). Because your children see you living happily as a "child of God," they grasp an important life-lesson—that prayer is part of grown-up life, not merely a charming childhood make-believe, like Santa Claus, that's later outgrown.

- Children delight in stories, and they acutely need heroes to pattern their lives after. So you tell them stories of Christ and his Blessed Mother and the Apostles, figures of the Old Testament, the heroism of the saints and missionaries. (If your children have no heroes, they pattern themselves after media "celebrities.")

- From time to time, you ask your children for their prayers, explaining that God loves children's prayers in a particular way. Children can't contribute many big things to family life, but their prayers are powerful before God. Let them see how much you value their prayers, how you and God are grateful for their prayers.

- You lead your children to pray for the Holy Father, for our bishops (successors of the Apostles), priests, and religious, the needs of the Church (especially religious vocations), and the needs of all, including our public leaders.

- You teach reverence for the Eucharist: dressing well for Mass, genuflecting reverently, preparing for Holy Communion—in short, exquisitely good manners toward Christ, who is with us as our greatest Friend. Make visits to the Blessed Sacrament just to say hello to Jesus in the tabernacle, who is all alone so much of the time.

- You teach your children to have recourse to Mary. The Rosary—or part of it, for small children—is a significant part of family life, a bedrock for the family's faith and hope. Because you earnestly beseech Mary thousands and thousands of times, "pray for us sinners, now and at the hour of our death," you are confident she will intercede with her Son to grant each of your children a great, adventurous life and a holy death.

- You show them your love for the sacrament of Reconciliation. Our Lord said that we must become like little children, and he grants us "spiritual childhood" with each good confession. No matter what wrong we have done, our sincere sacramental apology leads us to begin a new life— to recapture once again all the innocence and purity, the glad peace of mind, that we enjoyed as children.

- You insist on this flat rule for your home: "We will have nothing in this house that treats other people as mere things. Therefore, we exclude media presentations— Internet sites, TV, videos, video games, magazines, music lyrics, posters—that glorify pornography (or anything like it), gratuitous violence, coarseness, vulgarity, anything that degrades people and offends God." This you stick with, not simply to shield or protect your children, but rather to teach them your steel-hard moral principles and the reasons behind them.

- When your children are older, as adolescents or young adults going out on their own, you remind them of what you taught them since childhood: Remember, God is always with you. Don't do anything to offend him. We are confident that you will live by our Faith and moral principles, and our prayers go with you every day.

- Finally, you make clear to your children: The finest way you can honor and thank us, your parents, is to embrace our religious principles, live by them all your lives, and pass them on to our grandchildren as our family's sacred legacy.

As your children approach and grow through adolescence, remember this: Young people aren't looking for a set of rules to live by. What they're really looking for is a life to imitate. They ask themselves: Who lives a great life? Whom shall I be like?

If you love your children unconditionally, and if you strive to live a holy adventurous life, you will win your children's hearts. As the years pass, your heroic, happy life will be the pattern for their own.

Lighting up the way by your own example, teach your children how to live Christian charity. Tell them, and above all show them, that charity does not mean giving away old clothes or just dropping cash in a collection basket. Christian charity—the charity of Jesus and the saints—means mostly compassionate understanding and forgiveness.

In family life, insist on apologies and mercy. Make your children let others off the hook; forgive and forget—for we do not really forgive unless we also forget. Teach them that grudge-bearing eats away at us like burning acid; it corrodes the spiritual life and the bond of affection we must hold for others, starting with our family. Allow no gossip or backbiting in the home.

Lead them to help the needy and lonely with their prayers, alms, and time.

Teach them to pray, as Christ and the Apostles taught us, for our president and other civic leaders—for they too have souls, and their rightful authority comes from God. We may find their policies morally repugnant and may labor hard to remove them from office, but as Christians we pray for their conversion and salvation, and we bear them no personal ill will.

In affairs of the Church, take meticulous care to harbor no animus toward anyone, especially priests. Never speak ill of the clergy. Remember Paul's blistering exhortation in his letter to the Galations (5:19–24), his blast against the evils of "dissension" and "party spirit." If you perceive Church figures doing wrong, lead your children to pray for their souls; strive to snuff out scandal with your charity and apostolate.

Also vitally important: Beware of scandalizing your children with anything resembling a Pharisaic posture of religion—"I thank you, Lord, that I am not like the rest of men . . . "—that is, a set of pietistic practices rendered feckless and sterile, root and branch, by self-righteous contempt for others. If your children perceive a chasm between what you preach and what you practice, they will judge you a hypocrite. This is immensely perilous to their faith.

In short, let your heart always be guided by Christ's command that we must hate the sin, love the sinner.

Your charity, like Christ's, must be absolute. It must embrace everyone on earth, without exception.

By your living example and your word, teach your children your principled convictions about Christian family life, lessons engraved forever in their hearts.

What should your children remember all their lives and then pass on to their own children?—

- God loves each one of us more than all the fathers and mothers in the world love their children. Christ freely came to live among us and suffered and died for each and every one of us personally, by name. He longs for us to return his love for us, to love him back, and that's what we try to do.
- The noble ambition of Christian parents is this: that their children grow to become great men and women, faithful to their parents' principles; that brothers and sisters remain loyal friends for life and rejoin again as a family—together with their own families and friends—forever in heaven. This sacred ideal is worth any sacrifice.
- Christian charity means mostly compassionate understanding, willingness to forgive and forget, letting others off the hook, praying for one's enemies, serving others with our prayers and powers. In short, charity means to treat others the same way Christ treats us: to *pardon the unpardonable and love the unlovable.*
- Jesus pleads with us to forgive offenses, and he blesses those who make peace. Among the more beautiful words in family life are these: "I'm sorry. Please forgive me" . . . and then from the other, "I forgive you." This form of love is the bond of perfection.
- Nothing, absolutely nothing, is worse than sin. To break our friendship with God—that is, to break ourselves against his loving will—is the worst of all tragedies.
- Next to sin itself, and related to it, the worst mistake in life is not to trust God.
- Children should pass through life knowing that, no matter what happens, there are two places on earth where they can always get another chance: in the hearts of their parents and in the sacrament of Reconciliation.

⚓

As Pope John Paul II has explained it, our faith is essentially an anthropology. We trust the Church because we trust Jesus Christ.

Don't let your children perceive the Church as a merely human structure, a bureaucratic, worldwide society imposing "rules" and "prohibitions" on us. Don't tell them we must live a certain way because "the Church commands it" or because "the Church forbids it." This mistaken idea of the Church is a rickety foundation for your children's faith, a precarious means for their resisting evil throughout life. If they see the Church in this distorted way, as an impersonal rule-imposing institution, they may someday cast it aside.

Instead, teach them this:

It is not "the Vatican" that teaches and warns us; it is Christ himself. It is Christ speaking through his Church, his immortal instrument for life-giving faith, our sure path toward eternal life and a hundred-fold happiness here on earth. Our Church teaches what Christ taught, no more and no less. In the Eucharist, Jesus left us his body and blood, his soul and divinity. But his voice he left with Peter—with the Roman Pontiff, whoever he may be in each generation, and those bishops who enjoy communion with him. This he explicitly promised: "He who hears you, hears me."

Christ's enemies once challenged him with this significant question: "By what authority do you do these things?"—a repudiating challenge hurled at the popes and the Church down the ages, even to our own time. Jesus stymied his foes and hinted at his answer by responding, "Was the baptism of John [the Baptist] from God or from men?" Christ's reply sets forth the vital question for our own age: Is the pope's authority—is the Church's authority—from God or from men? In other words, is the Church divine in origin, or is it merely a man-made institution like any other? On this one question the whole world is divided in two. We Catholics believe in our Church's divine origin, and therefore in its authority to speak for Jesus Christ.

After his Resurrection, Jesus appeared to Peter and other Apostles in the upper room. All were there except Thomas, who (we might suppose) was wandering somewhere over-come with grief. When Thomas returned, he refused to believe what Peter and the others told him. Only later, when Christ reappeared and lovingly offered the physical proof Thomas demanded, would this Apostle turn his heart to believe. What was Thomas's real problem? Just this: Thomas would not believe Peter and the other Apostles; that is, he would not believe the Church. And what was Christ's lesson to Thomas and to us? It was this: Believe those to whom I said, "He who hears you, hears me."

In the name of Christ, the Church teaches what we need to live by for our salvation—and this instruction, seen superfi-cially, can come across as "rule-giving." Christ conferred to Peter and the Apostles the duty to teach "all that I have *com-manded* you." And this the Church does to this day, clearly and repeatedly. It's that important. It's a matter of life or death.

And in the name of Christ, the Church warns about sins— the turning of our will away from God—that threaten our eter-nal life. The term "eternal life" appears more than thirty times in the New Testament. Eternal life, along with the hundred-fold in this life, is why Christ came among us; that's why, through his Church, he warns us of perils in every age. It's that impor-tant. It's a matter of life or death.

To look at the issue another way: Our relationship to the Church is not one of mere "membership." It is, rather, the bond of love one finds in a family. It is, in essence, a love affair.

St. Catherine of Siena, one of the more influential women in Church history, said, "If you are what you should be, you will set the whole world ablaze." Indeed, if you are what you should be, you will set your family ablaze. In the years to come, the lives of your children will give glory to God.

Take your children by the hand, and lead them to visit Jesus in the tabernacle. Let them see how much each visit means to you, and tell them how much it means to Jesus.

Teach them that everything is in the tabernacle: strength, effectiveness, consolation, forgiveness, mercy, heartfelt love, a new beginning over and over again.

Explain how Jesus waits for visitors the same way he waited in the manger of Bethlehem. In the Sacred Eucharist, he lies waiting for us like the little baby he was on the first Christmas night: tiny, helpless, silent, still, wrapped in white, accompanied by a little fire, so easily approachable—and, as we say of tiny babies, utterly adorable.

Be sure of one thing. Your children will likely forget many of the details you taught them, but they will remember these childhood visits all their lives, and this poignant memory can save them. This remembrance can crack through the shell of any hard experience with life that afflicts them, that callus of the soul formed by life's troubles and sins and setbacks, so that the Holy Spirit can enter within their souls, then lead them to repentance, confession, and a new beginning.

Eucharistic piety fixed firmly in childhood has lifelong consequences.

Teach your children the virtue of gratitude, that most exquisite form of courtesy. Teach them to be truly grateful and to extend sincere thanks to others. This gratefulness is the swiftest, most powerful way to lead them out of their childish self-centeredness—"Me first!"—to an acute awareness of other people's dignity, rights, and sensibilities. Without this awareness and outward turning, they will never really grow up.

Teaching youngsters to say, and then *mean*, "please" and "thank you" is challenging. It takes stretches of seemingly endless correction and backsliding, months and often years of patient, valiant perseverance. The seeming futility of such labor—that is, high input but few apparent short-term results—is why so many fathers and mothers neglect this crucial duty or simply give up on it. Later, to their dismay, negligent parents suffer from their children's habitual, irreformable self-absorption—a bedrock egocentrism that undercuts their faith and damages or destroys their marriages.

Giving thanks to others is not only a social refinement or even an act of charity; it is a matter of justice, that is, giving others what is due them. Everything important in life comes to us from others, principally from our parents—life, health, home, food and clothing, education, parental and societal protection—and so we owe others our gratitude.

Look your children in the eye and press them to see how vitally important this is to you. A habit of gratefulness to Mom, Dad, and others will extend, among other great benefits, to the virtue of religion.

For it is ultimately God to whom we owe thanks. And this gratitude builds the basis for children's lifelong piety.

How so?

Gratitude makes us acutely aware that life is a gift. Even the ancient pagans, including our distant forebears, saw life this way, as a mysterious, gratuitous gift from some Higher Power. Indeed, our present age is the first in history where people fail to see life as gift. Our own neo-paganism strains instead to see life as a meaningless molecular accident, a dance of atoms that chance to fall into the phenomenon we call "life."

Gratitude leads us to see God as a person who loves us. It gives a heartfelt personal dimension to all aspects of living our faith.

Gratitude underscores the evil of sin. We see sin not merely as disobedience to a set of rules but rather as what it really is—a horrific offense to the One who loves us, an ungrateful rejection of his will and mercy, a heartless turning away from his friendship.

Gratitude makes the Mass come alive for us. We worship God to thank him for everything. Indeed the Greek word from which "Eucharist" comes means "to give thanks."

Gratitude leads us, and in a certain sense impels us, to heartfelt personal prayer. If we see our lives enriched by God's blessings, we feel the need to pray: We feel a joyful obligation to express our thanks by raising our minds and hearts to our heavenly Father.

Gratitude makes us see our adversities in perspective. All things considered, even with our hardships and setbacks, we enjoy a great life. And we're confident that God, who has showered us throughout life with his gifts, will also give us the strength and means to overcome anything. Christ, who saved us through his suffering, will unite our sufferings with his own for the redemption of mankind, including us and our loved ones.

Beauty, it is said, is composed partly of the idea that we are loved.

Beautiful things heighten our awareness that life is a gift. Beauty leads us to gratitude. Beauty leads us to God.

Therefore, direct your children's eyes to see beauty as you see it all around you. Lead them to appreciate, as you do, the beautiful things God blesses us with in normal life: affectionate family love, generosity and forgiveness, health, sports and games, fun with friends, meaningful work.

Lead them to see beauty, too, in the world God gave us: trees and flowers, the wondrous life of animals, clouds and sunsets, and the mysterious swirl of the heavens at night.

Teach them the beauties of great music, our sacred liturgy, exquisite art, splendid architecture, literary works that honor heroism and sacrificial achievement.

Goodness, truth, and beauty—these form the essence of what you should teach your children about the world they live in. Remember the words of Plutarch, "The mind is not a vessel to be filled, but a fire to be enkindled." Do not neglect the power of beauty, the awareness of life as a gift, to light the way of your children's lifelong search for God.

Don't let the miraculous in your life become humdrum. Don't let your sacramental life wind down, like a slackened mainspring, into dull routine. Think of the graces God showers upon you, and how much you and your family need them. Think how much you please God. And think how little time you have.

A priest was visiting a chapel far from his home, and he vested for Mass in its tiny sacristy. Glancing at the wall, his eyes rested on a little plaque, yellow from age, with this gentle but pointed message: "Father, say this Mass as if it were your first, . . . and say it as if it were your last."

Applied to us laypeople, this advice could be rephrased with equal wisdom: Take part in each Mass as if it were your very first, . . . and devour the prayers and the breathtaking, miraculous meaning of each Mass as if it were the last in your life. Someday, one of your Masses will be your last.

And so too for the sacrament of Reconciliation: Make each confession with the candid completeness and sincere repentance you would put into your last confession on earth. Someday, one of them will be your last.

St. Don Bosco, an expert in the patient nourishing of children's souls, described his life-outlook in these words, advice that can give heart to any Christian parent: "Do what you can. . . . God and our Lady will do the rest."

3.

Joyful Perseverance

To persevere in your vocation takes courage. To set yourself to your mission—never giving up, never even letting up—calls for a valiant, generous heart. Anyone who has striven and triumphed through a rich, adventurous life knows why this is so. Heart gives life's-blood to perseverance.

Courage, the very soul of adventure, springs to life from some great love. Courage means to give oneself, regardless of trials and obstacles, to another: to a soul, to one's family, to country, to God. Heartfelt love like that of saints and parents—above all, saintly parents—begets patient perseverance, risk-taking adventure, a faith that nothing can shake.

It is the common experience of humanity that self-absorbed pessimists never accomplish anything of worth. All of history's great achievements were brought to life by men and women with one thing in common: they were impelled forward, driven to surpass themselves, by the fire of some great passionate love.

So, reflect on this as you go about your daily life of patient and generous self-giving. In the pages of the Scriptures, inspired by the Holy Spirit, the word *heart* recurs more than a thousand times. God wants your courageous heart and, through you, the hearts of your children.

Your children are watching—so be joyful in your courage. Your children need to see you live this way, totally unafraid.

Don't be afraid of today's "moral environment." Don't let fear of the world—a monastic-like retreat from normal society—suffuse and set the tone for what you teach your children. Fear undercuts leadership. No one follows an uncertain trumpet.

Be optimistic, rather, and full of Christian hope. You must be a leader to your children, and all leadership is based on hope. Let your children know what evils await them, to be sure, but tell them you are confident, you have no doubt whatever, that they will do right and live right in all the pathways of their lives.

Teach them the vital distinction between love for the world, which is good, and worldliness, which is evil.

We Christians love the world because normal society is where God has placed us. This world, our way-station on our path to heaven, is where he has called us to live as his witnesses, his present-day apostles. God calls on us not to flee this world but to transform it—to make it holy, starting with ourselves.

Worldliness, on the other hand, is a lie. It is the godless belief that this world is all there is, this earthly life is all we have, for no life awaits us beyond the grave. Worldliness is another term for materialism, the twisted vision of life that we must shun.

Take courage from what Christian fathers and mothers in past ages, our forebears in the Faith, had to contend with and overcome.

In the early Church, Christian parents were surrounded by militant and aggressive forces of evil, constant threats to their children's souls. The ancient world routinely, almost casually, killed defective infants and newborn baby girls; female infanticide was commonplace and accepted. Contraception and abortion were taken for granted, even promoted by the finest minds of the time, men like Plato and Aristotle. Slavery, promiscuity, homosexuality, casual divorce, murderously violent games, public pornography, lewd theatre, cheating and exploitation of the poor, misunderstanding and contempt for the Faith—all this depravity flew in the face of Christian fathers and mothers as they struggled to raise their children.

Then later, over the course of centuries, still more adversities: enticing and aggressive heresies; scandalous lives among bishops, priests, and monks, even popes; schismatic confusion; shortage of holy priests and trustworthy teachers; violent persecution by political forces; social ostracism; unjust taxation; economic pressures to prosper by abandoning the Faith.

So, today's "moral environment" is nothing new. What St. Paul called the "dominion of darkness" is ever with us.

In the midst of normal society, without abandoning the world that God gave them, our Christian forebears survived these evils and passed the Faith on to their children. With their joyful confidence in God and his Church, the holy optimism of the saints, they triumphed with their sons and daughters—and with their friends and neighbors and fellow citizens.

So can you.

It's a granite fact of family life everywhere: to live one's mission as father or mother means sacrifice, that is, self-giving hardship. Every parent knows what this means: relentless effort, occasional sleepless nights, patches of tedium and fatigue, backsliding by the children, constant challenges to one's strength and patience and stamina.

But the history of human affairs shows one truth clearly, sometimes dramatically: without sacrifice, nothing of significance, nothing really worth doing, can be brought to completion.

From time to time, as you come to grips with your challenges in family life, remember Christ's words, "My yoke is easy, and my burden is light" (Mt 11:30)

To live as a parent means shouldering the yoke of commitment and bearing the burden of responsibility. Yoke and burden—they come with the mission God has given you.

But with your love for Jesus and your family, you will find joy and light and perseverance to your final victory. With Jesus at the center of your family's heart, your children will give glory to God.

57

Listen to the counsel of St. James in his letter to our forebears in the Faith, all normal people striving for holiness in their newfound religion, nearly all of them parents just like you: "Count it all joy . . . when you meet various trials, for you know that the testing of your faith produces steadfastness. And let steadfastness have its full effect, that you may be perfect and complete, lacking in nothing" (Jas 1:2–4).

Look closely at these words, for their meaning is wonderful. God calls you—and, through you, each of your children—to become a masterpiece, "perfect and complete, lacking in nothing."

But remember, no masterpiece unfolds into being overnight in a flash of creativity. Nor does it spring to existence without the driving force of some great love. Every great achievement takes years of patient effort, high ideals, and faith-filled perseverance.

Learn from some lessons of history how a masterpiece is really made . . .

As a middle-aged man, Michelangelo lay on his back atop a rickety wooden scaffold vaulting high above the floor of the Sistine Chapel. By flickering lamplight, he patiently daubed paints and wet plaster to give life, a few square inches at a time, to his ambitious artistic vision. He kept at this harsh, exhausting labor for four years. Thus did he create his breathtaking fresco masterpiece, the most famous ceiling in the world.

Ludwig van Beethoven, afflicted with ever-encroaching deafness, hunched over his piano day after day for months at a time, creating great music from the sparks of his genius. Between his teeth he clenched an ivory wand and held it for hours to the piano's sounding board so he could sense, albeit faintly, the sounds of the music begotten in his mind. His agonizing perseverance, lit by his gift from God, brought forth the masterpieces that still thrill us with their power and beauty.

The French painter Claude Monet lost much of his eyesight

toward the end of his life and could scarcely travel from his home and its patch of garden at Giverny. Confined as he was, this nearly blind old man labored to bring forth three hundred lustrous paintings, mostly of his garden and little pond, among them his most beautiful and famous creations.

The vast cathedrals of Europe, masterpieces of awe-inspiring grandeur, rose slowly from the earth and took shape through generations of faith-filled vision, centuries of immense, patient toil. As we look back from our own age of quick fixes and rapid results, we find it hard to grasp the perseverance of those faith-inspired souls. We find it hard to understand people who could labor all their lives on their great undone project, shaping and setting one stone block at a time, knowing they would never in their lifetime see the end results of their sacrifices.

Mozart said, "Love, love, love—that is the soul of genius."

Patience driven by passion, this is the secret of great achievement—for great artists and great parents.

Fearfulness, a pressing anxiety, a shrinking back in apprehension—these are people's normal reactions when they confront their responsibilities, the challenges of their mission.

Pope John Paul II once said that responsibility is a call by God for us to surpass ourselves, and this call is often fearsome. Even Jesus Christ, as he neared the horrific climax of his redemptive mission, collapsed to the ground at Gethsemane, writhing in tearful agony, wetting the earth with his sweat and blood. In response to his anguish, God the Father consoled him.

God consoles us too when we come face to face with the challenges of our mission. So often in the Scriptures we hear his words of courage: "Don't be afraid!"

The angel Gabriel, sent to announce Mary's vocation, said to her, "Don't be afraid."

St. Joseph was told in a dream, "Don't be afraid to take Mary as your wife. . . ."

When Jesus worked the miraculous catch of fish and called Peter to his life's mission of fishing for men, he said, "Don't be afraid. . . ."

In the dramatic episode of the storm on the lake, and later when he walked on the water, Jesus admonished his disciples, Peter above all, not to be afraid.

Jesus told his followers not to fear those who can harm the body—rather, to fear only those who can harm the soul, thrust it into hell.

After his Resurrection, Christ appeared to his friends and set their souls at peace by saying, "Don't be afraid."

And so he says to you, as you come face to face with your own holy mission, your family responsibilities, "Don't be afraid! . . . Nothing shall be impossible to God."

It has wisely been said: Anxiety doesn't solve problems tomorrow; it only empties today of its strength.

From time to time, as you face the challenges of forming your children for life, ask yourself two key questions in the presence of God:

> What are you really afraid of?
> What could you accomplish if you lost those fears?

Learn from the example of those valiant women who set out on Easter morning to anoint the body of Jesus. They had no idea how they could shove aside the massive stone sealing Jesus' grave, a seemingly impossible problem. Yet they pushed on, impelled by the courage of their love for Jesus, confident that somehow they would succeed. And so they triumphed.

The lesson for you: Love overcomes fear. A great love can overcome anything.

Listen to the words of St. Josemaría Escrivá, a holy spiritual director to countless souls:

"You are suffering a great tribulation? You have reverses? Say very slowly, as if savoring it, this powerful and virile prayer: 'May the most just and most lovable will of God be done, be fulfilled, be praised and eternally exalted above all things. Amen. Amen.' I promise you that you will find peace" (*The Way*, no. 691).

Picture this scene from the Gospels. Jesus is teaching his disciples in the Temple at Jerusalem, that splendid site of sacrificial offering built by Solomon, his forebear in the line of David, for the worship and glory of God. A poor widow, full of faith in God, approaches the offering chest, stretches out her hand, and drops in two little copper coins.

Jesus, his face radiant with gladness, points her out to his disciples and says to them—and to all of us down the ages—". . . this poor widow has put in more than all those who are contributing to the treasury. For they all contributed out of their abundance; but she out of her poverty has put in everything she had, her whole living."

To be truly "poor in spirit," to embrace the Christian virtue of poverty, means this: to put *all* our trust in God.

Generosity means, among other things, a risk-taking moved by love. Generosity means sacrifice, and sacrifice is another term for love.

In the pages of the Gospels, Jesus seems to attract generous people and to bring out the best in them. He seems to delight in people's generosity, and even to depend on it. Think of these examples . . .

St. Joseph, returning to Judea from the flight into Egypt, had apparently planned to settle down and set up shop in Bethlehem. But Archelaus, Herod's successor, posed a danger to his family, and so Joseph turned aside to live in Nazareth—a village so insignificant that Nathaniel, at a later time, would dismiss it with scorn. Joseph changed his plans and sacrificed his "career ambitions" to protect his wife and son. Good father that he was, he put his family first.

The Apostles, for all their faults, left their nets and boats—everything they had—to follow Jesus.

Matthew, a wealthy tax-collector and despised outcast among his fellow Jews, abandoned all his riches at Jesus' call.

Simon Peter, exhausted from a night's fruitless fishing, made his boat available for Jesus to preach to crowds huddling on the shore. Then, when Jesus finished and Peter thought he could at last return home to sleep, Jesus pressed him to fish again, to set aside his weariness and push out into the deep. Peter, though worn out, trusted Jesus and did as he wished. (A trusting obedience, as parents know, is often the highest form of generosity.) The miracle that followed was so dramatic it altered the course of Peter's life, and our own lives too.

A Roman centurion, a good and generous man, built the synagogue in Capernaum in which Jesus announced his own great gift to mankind, his sacred presence in the Eucharist. The physical setting for Jesus' gift was itself a gift from this generous Gentile, a man of the type praised by the angels in Bethlehem, a man of good will.

Lazarus, Martha, and Mary extended their heartfelt hospitality to Jesus, throwing open their home to the great Friend who had nowhere to lay his head.

A young boy, a friend of the Apostle Andrew, willingly handed over to Jesus his lunch of loaves and fishes, a meal probably packed by his mother, simply because the Master asked him for it. Christ, in his turn, used this boy's generous gift to feed a crowd of thousands, including, of course, the boy himself.

Zaccheus, a sinner attracted to Jesus perhaps (we can guess) by a hopeful longing for forgiveness, joyfully received the gift of Christ's company in his home—and then gratefully, generously reformed his life.

Nicodemus and Joseph of Arimathea, secret disciples of Jesus, threw their reputation to the winds, committed social suicide, by coming to the aid of Mary at the death of her son, their Savior. Joseph swiftly, generously, gave his own tomb, carved out of rock and therefore expensive, to Jesus for his final burial.

So, remember Christ's words whenever he calls on you to be generous, risk-taking, self-sacrificing in your family adventure: "Give, and it will be given to you; good measure, pressed down, shaken together, running over, will be put into your lap. For the measure you give will be the measure you get back" (Lk 6:38)

Jesus also seemed to have a special place in his heart for pushy people—people moved to daring effort by a faith-inspired love, people who would not take "no" for an answer.

Recall the Gospel scene where Jesus is preaching within a house thronged by an overflow crowd (Mk 2:1–12). A group of four men approach; on a litter they carry a friend of theirs who is paralyzed. The crowd obstructs their passage, thwarts them from drawing near to Jesus to beseech a cure for their friend.

But this obstacle does not deter them. They are men of action and do not give up. They make their way around the house and, with great effort, hoist the litter up to the roof. They tear away the roof's tiles and timber and tenderly lower their friend by ropes to the feet of Christ. Jesus is their only hope, their friend's only hope, and so they won't take "no" for an answer.

The Gospel tells us Christ's reaction: "And when Jesus saw their faith, he said to the paralytic, 'My son, your sins are forgiven.'" Then, "I say to you, rise, take up your pallet and go home." Jesus uses his power over physical nature, which all can see, to show his power over the invisible—his power to forgive sins. As he can cure paralyzed limbs, so can he cure a paralyzed soul.

But notice the preface to this dramatic miracle: "When

Jesus saw *their* faith . . ." Jesus is moved to miracles, including miracles of grace, not only by the faith of the afflicted but also by the faith of their loved ones. Jesus responds to our ceaseless prayers and sacrifices for the cure of those we love.

Teach your children to pray for each other, not just now but throughout their lives. If one of your children should someday be grievously afflicted, blinded and wounded by entanglement in sin, your prayers and those of your other children can move Jesus to a miracle. Seeing *your* faith, he will work his cure.

St. Francis of Assisi once gave this holy advice to people faced with "impossible" problems: "Begin to do what's necessary, then do what's possible, and soon you are doing the impossible."

When parents open their hearts to welcome the souls God wills to send them, they are often rewarded with many children. God answers their generous faith by entrusting new souls to their care, new lives to nurture, teach, and lead back to him.

God smiles on open-hearted, adventurous parents like these and showers them with his never-failing help. He uses their busy, rollicking family life to strengthen each child in faith and virtue. Through the parents' sacrifices, he makes of each family a cadre of valiant, strong, self-confident men and women who will carry the Faith forward in history and influence those souls along their ways whose lives will intertwine with their own.

If you have been blessed with many children, you should thank God for this great honor and be confident of his never-failing help.

For your own peace of mind, too, you should pause now and then to think how your family life—busy and challenging as it often is—works to build up the faith and character of your children, and thereby the Church of the next generation. A large family is inherently formative; it's an ongoing apprenticeship in right living and leadership. Over the years it works to turn out young people who are empowered to surpass their contemporaries, succeed in their affairs, and emerge in life as leaders.

Consider how your family life benefits each of your sons and daughters. Through the give-and-take of growing up with several brothers and sisters, how are your children empowered to become better men and women? What happens is this . . .

- Because money and time and resources are in constant short-supply, the parents fervently rely on God's help. Mom and Dad turn often to God and lead their children to join them. Thus a spirit of trusting prayer suffuses family life, and God dwells in the heart of the family.
- Unlike most youngsters today, children in big families are genuinely needed at home. No "busy work" for them. Through their chores and handling of responsibilities around the house, they contribute to the family's welfare. That is, every day they practice putting their powers up against problems for the benefit of others. Consequently, they grow in self-knowledge (their strengths and limitations) and realistic self-confidence. They grow more mature more quickly. After all, the term *maturity* really means responsibility; maturity *is* responsibility.
- Consequently, they internalize the real meaning of responsibility—that is, *if we don't do our duty, someone we love will suffer.* So their moral development—moving from "self" to "others"—takes root more firmly. They grow to be givers, not takers.
- Surrounded by siblings' conversation and playful interaction, even including disagreements, they enjoy constant intellectual stimulation. This daily experience strengthens and sharpens their judgment.
- Even their normal squabbles and spats, when refereed by parents, teach children lessons of fairness, sharing, splitting differences, letting others off the hook, forgiving and

forgetting. These lessons fortify their moral standards, their lifelong conscience. (Friction, though tedious and irksome at times, has its uses; it rounds off rough edges, forms a smooth, resilient surface.)

- They're surrounded by laughter. By and large, even with its ups and downs, the home of a large family is a happy place, a site of healthy fun. Good cheer, it seems, is livelier, more heartfelt, when shared with a crowd. All their lives, children from a large family remember the fun they had growing up together, the laughter and sheer delight of being alive and surrounded by love.

- Because their parents take care of their needs but cannot satisfy their whims (through lack of money and time), children learn the vital difference between wants and needs. They learn to wait for what they want, or to work and earn it themselves. Thus they escape the corruptive influence of instant gratification. They internalize the virtues of patience and honorable ambition. They grow to become resourceful self-starters.

- Through interactions with their siblings, enlightened by the parents' teaching, children more deeply understand gender differences. From their sisters, boys understand and appreciate the beautiful qualities of femininity; from their brothers, girls understand and appreciate what's common and admirable among males. With the light of these insights, all the children are better prepared for dating, courtship, and marriage.

- One of the mysteries of a large family is the startling differences children display in temperaments, talents, and interests. By dealing with these differences among their brothers and sisters, the children learn to get along with anyone. Having to share a bedroom and bathroom and space at the table prepares children superbly for marriage and for life.

- Older children play with the youngest ones and thus form a bond of affection with them, an apprenticeship for parenthood. Younger children receive love and learning from an array of older people, not only their parents. So older children are pulled out of their egos, and younger ones are enveloped by love.

- As the years pass, each child journeys through life enjoying the support of his grown-up brothers and sisters. No matter what befalls them later in life, your children will never be alone. Indeed, the finest gift parents can give their children, the gift lasting a lifetime, is their brothers and sisters.

Pause from time to time to think of the good in your children: the gifts and goodness God placed in their souls, as well as the good you see growing within them.

Your children's flaws and occasional flare-ups, all stark evidence of original sin, are the raw material for your efforts to correct them. And, of course, you must make those efforts when necessary.

But don't forget, children's faults are so annoying to us that we tend to exaggerate them, blow them out of proportion, sometimes overreact to them. This is why it's important to balance your perspective, see your children as they really are, see what's good in them.

Remember, most of the time your children are well disposed and well behaved. What's more, small children have beautiful qualities that we, the adults in their lives, need to learn from and cultivate within ourselves. For instance . . .

Once instructed in our religion, they swiftly outdo us in faith and piety. Truly, all of us adults can learn from the powerful faith and prayers of little children.

They are incredibly resilient; they bounce back quickly from adversity.

They do not bear grudges. Though they're often quick to forget correction (a lapse that annoys us), they're also quick to forgive and forget transgressions. Apology works with them. They have a capacity for mercy.

To them, work and play are one. When they're very young, sheer effort is part of their joy in being alive. They delight in being needed; in some sense, they need to be needed.

They have a steady gaze on the truth. They see life flat on, and they say what they think.

So, remind yourself of all these things as you go about forming your children: to correct what needs correcting and to preserve for life what needs preserving.

Michelangelo was once asked how he went about sculpting a massive marble block into one of his sublime masterpieces, a magnificent angel. He said, "I saw the angel in the marble, and I carved until I set him free."

It is a fact that your children, as they grow through adolescence into young adulthood, will confront temptations poised against their faith and their purity of heart. Do not be afraid of this. If you have prayed and labored to teach them right from wrong, to give sinews to their consciences for life, they will be empowered, with God's help, to triumph.

Take courage from these stirring words of Christ—a peroration of hope—at the conclusion of St. Mark's Gospel (Mk 16:17–18):

> And these signs will accompany those who believe: in my name they will cast out demons, . . . they will pick up serpents, and if they drink any deadly thing, it will not hurt them. . . .

It's certain that your children will meet with demons who entice them to evil, but in Jesus' name—in prayer and confession—they will cast the demons out of their lives.

As teens and young adults, they will meet sly serpents who will tempt them, but these they will handle as you have taught them to do. Through the power of their conscience, they will thrust the serpents aside and, with Mary's help, crush their heads.

They will encounter godless people, attractive and cunning,

who will try to poison their minds. As Montaigne wrote, "The reverse of truth has a thousand shapes." But with the Faith you taught them since infancy, they will know falsehood when they see it, and they will remain unharmed.

Every single step you take now, no matter how small, to teach your children to love God and flee sin will bear fruit in your children's souls for life. Remember the words of St. Paul (Gal 6:9): "Let us not grow weary in well-doing, for in due season we shall reap, if we do not lose heart."

Someone wisely observed, "We tend to become what we think about." Our life-experience shows this is true, doesn't it?

Those who center their thoughts on money become well-off.

Those who set out to sway human affairs become influential.

Those who think only of comfort become feckless layabouts.

Those obsessed with pleasure become predatory beasts.

Those who worship themselves and their interests become godless.

But this dynamic works in other ways, too, ways that parents should hold before them as they go about their sacred mission.

Parents who think of service to their family become beloved leaders.

Parents who think of children's moral growth become the voice of their children's conscience.

Parents who set out to give good example become their children's guides for life.

Parents who center their hearts on their mission become their children's heroes.

Parents who think of Christ become Christlike in act and outlook.

Parents who think of loving service to God, and then act that way, become saints.

Johann Goethe said, "We are shaped and fashioned by what

we love." If you, despite your faults, lead your children to love Jesus Christ as you try to—with all your heart and soul and mind and strength—you will let the Holy Spirit shape and fashion your family toward the holiness of the saints.

The great theologian Eusebius once wrote, "You cannot really pray unless you are willing to die." To this truth we might add: You cannot really pray unless you are willing to wait.

The prophet Isaiah put it this way: ". . . the LORD waits to be gracious to you; therefore he exalts himself to show mercy to you. For the LORD is a God of justice; blessed are all those who wait for him" (Is 30:18).

God always answers our prayers. Always. But sometimes his answer is, "Not yet." Sometimes, for reasons known only to him, God makes us wait.

God's plan for our welfare, like any human plan of action, calls for appropriate timing. There's a fit time for everything, and this sometimes means waiting. Remind yourself often: *God knows what he is doing.*

You've seen this in your own family life, haven't you? For instance, a half-hour before dinner, your hungry child pleads for a snack. Your answer is, of course, "Not yet. Be patient. You'd ruin your appetite. First you have to get through dinner, then comes the dessert." What your children want and what they need—that is, what is good for them—are two different things. When children must wait for things, they grow stronger, more patient and persevering. Time is, after all, a resource; waiting teaches all of us, adults as well as children, the power of trusting perseverance and persevering prayer.

Don't impose your timetable on God. He knows what he is doing.

But there's a shortcut you can take to move things along, an approach used by Christians from the earliest days of the

Church: Appeal to the Mother of God. Ask Mary to intercede for you.

Mary is the specialist on those domestic problems, large and small, that weigh on parents' peace of mind, for she has a mother's heart.

See how she discreetly approached Jesus at the wedding feast in Cana and pressed him to alter his timetable, his own plan for working the first miracles in his public life, whatever these were to be. For the sake of her friends, a young married couple, Mary pleaded with her son to spare them social embarrassment on this once-in-a-lifetime occasion, their wedding day, when (as every woman knows) every detail must be perfect and memorable.

Jesus replied, quite reasonably, "My time has not yet come." But, good mother that she is, she would not give up. She took direct action, as all great women do, and put him on the spot. She sent the stewards to her son, saying to them (and to all of us down the ages), "Do whatever he tells you."

We know the rest. Jesus worked his first miracle then, and not later, because he could not refuse his mother. This was the lesson Christ left us: Mary is your mother as well as mine, and she has a special "in" with me. Pray to me through her and I will shorten your wait—I will not refuse you.

Ask the Holy Spirit to cultivate within you the gift of wisdom. This is the power to discern what's important from what's not.

It was Goethe who said, "Things that matter most must never be at the mercy of things that matter least."

A curious thing often happens when young mothers and fathers, striving to do the right thing with their small children, ask advice of older, "veteran" parents. The new parents earnestly pose questions, often in great detail, about the puzzles and uncertainties that vex them every day: What's age-appropriate? What's normal? What kind of discipline fits a certain crisis-situation, and how can you tell? How do you deal with sulkiness, wildness, resistance to correction, sibling rivalry, and on and on?

To all these earnest queries, how do the experienced parents respond? Usually they reach back into their memory of trial and error and recount what worked with them.

But sometimes, very often in fact, they respond differently: with a mildly dismissive shrug or wave of the hand, a wry smile of recognition and remembrance. They're amused to see once again the minutely detailed concerns that they also used to worry about before they learned better. "Don't worry so much about that," they say. "You're worrying too much about nitty-gritty details. You should focus instead on what's important." Through their years of experience, they've grown to see what's important and what's not. That is, they have wisdom.

If you asked such veterans (as I have) what they've found to be really important in raising children right, here are some lessons they'd pass on to you:

- Don't look for recipes or fixed formulas for raising children. There are none. And don't expect perfection from your spouse, your children, or yourself. Instead, set a realistic ideal for your children as responsible Christian adults, and then strive to work toward that ideal together with your spouse in ongoing, unified parental leadership.
- Be confident of your rightful authority—which derives from your huge, God-given responsibility—and insist that your children respect it.
- Remind yourself often: you're raising adults, not children.
- Have faith in later results; see your sacrifices as investment that will pay off later.
- When you think of your children's futures, picture their character, not simply their careers. Set out to teach the great character strengths: sound judgment, a sense of responsibility, courageous perseverance, self-mastery, faith, hope, and charity.
- Give your children time and affection, not money.
- Teach your children the four great pillars of civilized deal-

ings with others: "please," "thank you," "I'm sorry," and "I give my word . . ."

- Teach your children to pray, mostly by letting them join you in talking with God. Ask them to pray for you and your intentions. Let their prayers, based on your example, center on "please," "thank you," "I'm sorry," and "I give my word . . ."—all of which mean, as in family life, "I love you."

- Remember, the whole of moral development means moving from *self* to *others*. Your children will not grow up when they can take care of themselves; they will grow up only when they can take care of others, and want to.

- Teach them what real love means: sacrifice—including risk-taking—for the welfare of others. Lead your children to honor and appreciate your spouse, as you do. Keep at this for years.

- Show your older children how to work well; don't do their work for them unless and until they've tried their best. Push for personal best effort, not merely results.

- Make your children wait for something big they want, and if possible make them earn it.

- Make your children feel needed and appreciated; make praise as specific as blame, and just as sincere.

- Whenever you have something important to teach your children, look them in the face. Let them perceive in your eyes (the windows of the soul) the depth of your convictions and your loving confidence in them.

- Teach your children the meaning of the word integrity. Integrity means unity of intention, word, and action. We mean what we say, we say what we mean, and we keep our word. Trust their integrity, even if you must sometimes mistrust their judgment, and teach them this distinction.

- Show them how to recognize materialism when they see it, and to shun it. Materialism is not merely the pursuit of things. It means putting things ahead of people. It leads to *seeing and treating other people as things.*

- Keep the media under your discerning control. Allow nothing in your home that offends God, undermines your lessons of right and wrong, and treats other people as mere objects.

- Lead your children to practice Christian charity, which means mostly compassionate understanding. In family life, insist on apologies and forgiveness. Here as elsewhere, lead by example.

- Teach your older children to set goals and manage their time—that is, to control themselves. If children cannot set and meet goals, they cannot set and meet ideals.

- Cultivate family honor, the spirit of "We . . ." Let the rules of your home begin with "We . . . " That is, the house rules are for everyone in the family, not only for the children. (For instance, "We return things where they belong, . . . We call if we're going to be late, . . . We apologize if we've caused offense.")

- Let your children know what's expected of them. Make standards and consequences clear.

- Listen to your children. That's *listen*, not obey. Let children contribute "input" to family life—but in serious matters, you make the decisions.

- Where appropriate, give your children "loving denial"—for "no" is as much a loving word as "yes." If children don't hear "no" from their parents when appropriate, they cannot say "no" to themselves. The power of self-mastery is built from the outside in.

- In matters of discipline, practice "affectionate assertiveness." Correct the fault, not the person; hate the sin, love the sinner. Show your children you love them too much to let them grow up with their faults uncorrected.

- Treat punishment as "memorable correction"—action needed now to avert later troubles and sorrow, maybe even tragedy. After the children apologize and make amends, welcome them back affectionately to your good graces.

- Take corrective action without showing disrespect. Respect your children's rights as people.

- Save your outrage for what's truly outrageous. Otherwise your children won't learn what's outrageous.

74

- Don't let your pride come ahead of truth or justice; when you've made a mistake or gone too far, apologize.
- Don't let your children infringe on the rights of others. Remember, the way they treat their siblings now is an apprenticeship for the way they'll later treat spouse, children, colleagues, and others in their lives.
- Make dinner a sacred time: no quarrels or squabbling allowed. Start dinner with a prayer.
- In matters of morality, teach them indifference to being thought "different."
- Don't let organized sports fracture family life. Busyness is not a virtue. Athletics should bring cheerful calm and energy to young people, not frantic exhaustion. Cut back to what's healthy and reasonable, and make better use of the few years you have together as a family.
- Keep your priorities straight: When you're upset by a problem, ask yourself: "How important will this be a year from now, five years from now, or even next month?"
- Be affectionate with your children. Do this frequently and on purpose. Your children will return all their lives—including in their memory—to the place where they knew affection.
- Remember that your children may forget most of the details of what you teach them, but they will remember what was *important* to you. For most of us, the lifelong voice of conscience is the voice of our parents—God speaking to us through the memory of what our parents lovingly taught us.
- Treat your children the way God treats all of us: with high standards, loving protection, great hopes for the future, affectionate understanding, readiness to forgive, and never-failing love.

Robert Hugh Benson once said, "We are responsible for doing what we can. . . . To see and dream without the power of performance is heartbreaking."

He was touching on a truth of the human experience: to risk is to live. To be alive—that is, really to live life to its fullest—is to take risks, to commit yourself daringly to an adventure. All great figures in history, including the great saints, lived this way. They propelled their lives forward by putting their ideals into action.

Think of this. If you visited terminally ill people as they lay on their deathbeds and asked them what they would have done differently with their lives, most would probably say, "I wish I'd taken more risks."

No one on his deathbed, about to come face to face with God, should have to say, like the servant who buried his talent, "I'm glad I played it safe."

If you persevere in your vocation, you will be able to say what St. John exclaimed in a heartfelt letter to the early Christians, "I have no greater joy than this: to know that my children are walking in the truth."

God made us to know him, to love him, and to serve him—and to do all this freely, by an act of our will. We received a life's mission from God in order to consent to it. We were born to consent.

Everything in the universe belongs to God. Everything, that is, but our will. Our own free will is the only thing we possess entirely, the only thing wholly in our power to give or withhold.

So the offering of our will to God—our consent to make his will our own—is the most perfect gift we can make to him.

The saints differed in many ways. They varied in talents and temperaments and ways of life. But what they all had in common was this: They sought to know God's will, to embrace it absolutely, and to center their lives on it.

Loving consent to the will of God is the essence of holiness.

There are times when God's will for us and our loved ones may seem hard to understand, harder still to accept. At such times, what should we do?

Listen to the counsel of a saint. With his great holiness and a lifetime spent directing souls, including countless parents, St. Josemaría Escrivá summed up his experience this way:

> With crystal clarity I see the formula, the secret of happiness, both earthly and eternal. It is not just a matter of accepting the will of God but of embracing it, of identifying oneself with it—in a word, of loving the Divine Will with a positive act of our own will.
>
> This, I repeat, is the infallible secret of joy and peace (*The Forge*, no. 1006).

St. Maximilian Kolbe was renowned among those who knew him for his radiant happiness and saintly serenity. His celebrated sacrifice at Auschwitz, where he surrendered his life to save another prisoner from execution, was a logical endpoint for the trajectory of his whole life, a life given joyfully to God and to others.

Once, a friend asked him what was the secret of happiness in life. He took a sheet of paper and wrote this equation: $w = W$.

He said, "The small w is my will. The capital W is the will of God. When my will is God's will, and when his is mine, the result is happiness."

In its deepest sense, contemplation means this: to seek to know the will of God and then to embrace it wholly and unconditionally. When we embrace God's will wholeheartedly, we experience the deepest joy and greatest inner peace that anyone can know.

Take heart from the accounts of two dramatic miracles in the Gospel.

In one case, the distraught father of a possessed boy approached Jesus and desperately pleaded, "If you can do anything, have pity on us and help us."

Jesus fixed on the father's words *if you can* and what they signified. He said, "If you can! All things are possible to him who believes." To which the father cried out in tears, "I do believe; help my unbelief!" Then Jesus worked his miracle; he expelled the demon and cured the man's son.

In the second case, a poor leper, a man afflicted with a repulsive and incurable disease, approached Jesus, fell on his knees, and pleaded, "If you will, you can make me clean." Then Jesus, moved with compassion, stretched forth his hand and touched him, saying, "I will; be made clean."

See the difference in faith? If you *can* . . . if you *will* . . .

We must be firmly confident, not simply that God *can* work his miracles but that he *will*. Each of us can repeat the prayer of the distraught father, "I do believe; help my unbelief." That is, give me the complete, wholehearted, abandoning trust of the poor leper: "If you will, you can make me clean."

Think of St. Joseph, the husband of Mary. What a splendid model for loving, responsible fatherhood! He never says a word in the Gospels, but he was a man of sacrificial action, a "just man." Consider what he went through.

His marriage plans are thrown awry when he finds that Mary, his espoused, is with child. In a dream he learns the truth of his vocation and takes Mary as his ever-virginal wife.

Obeying a political edict, he arrives in Bethlehem at the worst possible time for his family, with his wife about to give birth. As hard as he searches, filled with growing apprehension, he can find no decent private place for this sacred event.

When the Magi arrive to worship his baby son in Bethlehem, Joseph is not mentioned as being present, in Matthew's account. Later, warned in a dream, he arises at once from bed and takes his family swiftly to Egypt for their protection.

When he returns with them, he is warned again about the perils of living in Judea. So, abandoning his plans to settle there, he presses on to the obscure village of Nazareth in Galilee, where his family will be safe.

A good Jewish father, he leads Jesus in prayer and teaches him the holy Scriptures—the word of God prophesying salvation from the great Messiah, this little one who sleeps in his arms and works beside him.

As Jesus grows to manhood, Joseph's mission as protector and provider comes to completion—and he returns home to God, welcomed as a good and faithful servant, the model of a manly, saintly father.

What is the lesson for you in Joseph's silent life of service? What can you learn from the way Joseph lived his vocation? Just this . . .

When you are anxious and burdened with the weight of your family responsibilities . . .

When you feel the press of financial obligations and don't know how you'll meet them . . .

When your carefully constructed plans are upended by unforeseen crises . . .

When your life is tossed around by political decisions from on high . . .

When you must sacrifice your ambitions and interests for the welfare of your children . . .

When powerful forces threaten your family . . .

When bad things are happening to you and you don't know why . . .

Then go to St. Joseph. He understands. As a father, he has "been there." And Jesus, now in heaven, just as when he lived in the holy house of Nazareth, will never deny any request that Joseph asks of him.

If we dedicate ourselves to know and love Jesus Christ more each day—to see his face and devoutly thank him for his love for us, then serve him by serving those around us—then gradually, mysteriously, we become Christlike ourselves. Not completely, to be sure, but enough to make a difference. We see our life as Christ sees it. We treat others as he would treat them. We grow in the life of the Beatitudes, such that we can say with St. Paul, "It is no longer I who live, but Christ who lives in me."

If we welcome Jesus Christ inside our lives, then he will shape and fashion us as he willed from all eternity—and lead our children to become great men and women.

One final thought.

An ancient adage tells us, "As the day goes, so goes one's life." That is, the tenor and direction of each day, one day at a time, determines the course of one's whole life. Those who plod aimlessly through each day will plod aimlessly through life. Those who meet risky challenges each day with a sporting spirit will enjoy a life of adventurous achievement. And those who seek to please God each day by serving others will live a life that gives glory to God.

One day at a time—that's how we build a great life and a great family.

As you go about the adventure of normal family life each day, with all its challenges, you may find courage and confidence from saying a beautiful prayer attributed to Pope Clement XI. Because it embraces all of life, it has been known for three centuries as the "Universal Prayer." It is addressed to God personally, and it is an inspiring "morning offering" in gratitude to God. Rely on it as you would a compass to set the bearing for each day right—and thus for your whole life and that of your children in the years to come:

> Lord, I believe in you: increase my faith. I trust in you: strengthen my trust. I love you: let me love you more and more. I am sorry for my sins: deepen my sorrow.
>
> I worship you as my first beginning, I long for you as my last end, I praise you as my constant helper, and call on you as my loving protector.
>
> Guide me by your wisdom, correct me with your justice, comfort me with your mercy, protect me with your power.

I offer you, Lord, my thoughts, to be fixed on you; my words, to have you for their theme; my actions, to reflect my love for you; my sufferings, to be endured for your greater glory.

I want to do what you ask of me: in the way you ask, because you ask it.

Lord, enlighten my understanding, strengthen my will, purify my heart, and make me holy.

Help me to repent of my past sins and to resist temptation in the future. Help me to rise above my human weakness and to grow stronger as a Christian.

Let me love you, my Lord and my God, and see myself as I really am: a pilgrim in this world, a Christian called to respect and love all whose lives I touch, those in authority over me or those under my authority, my friends and my enemies.

Help me to conquer anger with gentleness, greed by generosity, apathy by fervor. Help me to forget myself and reach out toward others.

Make me prudent in planning, courageous in taking risks. Make me patient in suffering, unassuming in prosperity.

Keep me, Lord, attentive at prayer, temperate in food and drink, diligent in my work, firm in my good intentions.

Let my conscience be clear, my conduct without fault, my speech blameless, my life well ordered.

Put me on guard against my human weaknesses. Let me cherish your love for me, keep your law, and come at last to your salvation.

Teach me to realize that this world is passing, that my true future is the happiness of heaven, that life on earth is short, and the life to come eternal.

Help me to prepare for death with a proper fear of judgment, but a greater trust in your goodness. Lead me safely through death to the endless joy of heaven.

Grant this through Christ our Lord. Amen.

4.

Confidence in God's Promises

The sublime passages gathered here, all taken from the Old and New Testaments, carry special meaning for Christian parents. They convey God's affectionate promises to his beloved children down the ages—promises of hope, love, faith, a great life, and eternal salvation.

As you savor these words and their meaning, reflect on this reality . . .

God spoke these promises in his Sacred Scriptures to give hope and encouragement to ordinary laypeople just like you. The Holy Spirit directed these hope-filled words, not to prophets and priests and holy religious, but to untold millions of men and women, fathers and mothers with growing children and family challenges just like your own.

As the drama of God's salvation played out through the centuries—springing from a pastoral chosen people, through Christ's coming among us, and now through his People of God, our Church—God's promises have given light and hope to every generation of parents and children. And now they can give the same light and hope to you.

Read these promises slowly and hopefully. God addresses them to you. He counts on you to take them within your heart and then place them in the heart of each of your children.

> My child, be attentive to my words,
> Incline your ear to my sayings.
> Let them not escape from your sight;
> keep them within your heart;
> For they are life to him who finds them,
> and healing to all his flesh.
>
> —*Proverbs 4: 20–22*

YOUR SACRED MISSION AS A PARENT

"Fear not, for I have redeemed you;
I have called you by name: you are mine."

—*Isaiah 43:1*

For I know the plans I have for you, says the LORD, plans for welfare and not for evil, to give you a future and a hope. Then you will call upon me and come and pray to me, and I will hear you. You will seek me and find me; when you seek me with all your heart, I will be found by you, says the LORD, and I will restore your fortunes. . . .

—*Jeremiah 29:11–13*

[God] saved us and called us with a holy calling, not in virtue of our works but in virtue of his own purpose and the grace which he gave us in Christ Jesus ages ago, and now has manifested through the appearing of our savior Christ Jesus, who abolished death and brought life and immortality to light through the Gospel. . . .

—*2 Timothy 1:9–11*

Finally, brethren, whatever is true, whatever is honorable, whatever is just, whatever is pure, whatever is lovely, whatever is gracious, if there is any excellence, if there is anything worthy of praise, think about these things. What you have learned and received and heard and seen in me, do; and the God of peace will be with you.

—*Philippians 4:8–9*

For this very reason make every effort to supplement your faith with virtue, and virtue with knowledge, and knowledge with self-control, and self-control with steadfastness, and steadfastness with godliness, and godliness with brotherly affection, and brotherly affection with love. For if these things are yours and abound, they keep you from being ineffective or unfruitful in the knowledge of our Lord Jesus Christ.

—*2 Peter 1:5–8*

But the steadfast love of the LORD is from everlasting to
    everlasting
  upon those who fear him,
  and his righteousness to children's children,
to those who keep his covenant
  and remember to do his commandments.

                  —Psalm 103:17–18

"I do not pray that thou shouldst take them out of the world
but that thou shouldst keep them from the evil one."

                           —John 17:15

  Do not accustom your mouth to lewd vulgarity,
    for it involves sinful speech.
  Remember your father and mother
    when you sit among great men;
  lest you be forgetful in their presence,
    and be deemed a fool on account of your habits;
  then you will wish that you had never been born,
    and you will curse the day of your birth.
  A man accustomed to use insulting words
    will never become disciplined all his days.

                  —Sirach 23:13–15

This is my covenant with them, says the LORD: my spirit which
is upon you, and my words which I have put in your mouth,
shall not depart out of your mouth, or out of the mouth of your
children, or out of the mouth of your children's children, says
the LORD, from this time forth and for evermore.

                    —Isaiah 59:21

"For this reason a man shall leave father and mother and
be joined to his wife, and the two shall become one flesh."
This mystery is a profound one, and I mean in reference to
Christ and the church. However, let each one of you love
his wife as himself, and let the wife see that she respects
her husband.

                  —Ephesians 5:31–33

House and wealth are inherited from fathers,
  but a prudent wife is from the Lord.
> —*Proverbs 19:14*

A woman's beauty gladdens the countenance,
  and surpasses every human desire.
If kindness and humility mark her speech,
  her husband is not like other men.
He who acquires a wife gets his best possession,
  a helper fit for him and a pillar of support.
> —*Sirach 36:22–24*

If anyone does not provide for his relatives, and especially for his own family, he has disowned the faith and is worse than an unbeliever.
> —*1 Timothy 5:8*

Fathers, do not provoke your children, lest they become discouraged.
> —*Colossians 3:21*

Discipline your son, and he will give you rest;
  he will give delight to your heart.
> —*Proverbs 29:17*

Pamper a child, and he will frighten you;
  play with him, and he will give you grief.
Do not laugh with him, lest you have sorrow with him,
  and in the end you will gnash your teeth.
Give him no authority in his youth,
  and do not ignore his errors.
> —*Sirach 30:9–11*

Train up a child in the way he should go,
  and when his is old, he will not depart from it.
> —*Proverbs 22:6*

Children, obey your parents in everything, for this pleases
the Lord.

—*Colossians 3:20*

Stand by your covenant and attend to it,
    and grow old in your work.
Do not wonder at the works of a sinner,
    but trust in the Lord and keep at your toil;
for it is easy in the sight of the Lord
    to enrich a poor man quickly and suddenly.
The blessing of the Lord is the reward of the godly,
    and quickly God causes his blessing to flourish.
Do not say, "What do I need,
    and what prosperity could be mine in the future?'
Do not say, "I have enough,
    and what calamity could happen to me in the future?"
In the day of prosperity, adversity is forgotten,
    and in the day of adversity, prosperity is not
        remembered.
For it is easy in the sight of the Lord
    to reward a man on the day of death according to his
        conduct.

—*Sirach 11:20–26*

O son, help your father in his old age,
    and do not grieve him as long as he lives;
even if he is lacking in understanding, show forbearance;
    in all your strength do not despise him.
For kindness to a father will not be forgotten,
    and against your sins it will be credited to you;
in the day of your affliction it will be remembered in your
        favor;
    as frost in fair weather, your sins will melt away.
Whoever forsakes his father is like a blasphemer,
    and whoever angers his mother is cursed by the Lord.

—*Sirach 3:12–16I*

If you are willing, my son, you will be taught,
　　and if you apply yourself you will become clever.
If you love to listen you will gain knowledge,
　　and if you incline your ear you will become wise.
Stand in the assembly of the elders.
　　Who is wise? Cleave to him.
Be ready to listen to every narrative,
　　and do not let wise proverbs escape you.
If you see an intelligent man, visit him early;
　　let your foot wear out his doorstep.
Reflect on the statues of the Lord,
　　and meditate at all times on his commandments.
　　　It is he who will give insight to your mind,
　　　　and your desire for wisdom will be granted.

—Sirach 6:32–37

Listen to me your father, O children;
　　and act accordingly, that you may be kept in safety.
For the Lord honored the father above the children,
　　and he confirmed the right of the mother over her sons.
Whoever honors his father atones for sins,
　　and whoever glorifies his mother is like one who lays up
　　　treasure.
Whoever honors his father will be gladdened by his own
　　　children,
　　and when he prays he will be heard.
Whoever glorifies his father will have long life,
　　and whoever obeys the Lord will refresh his mother;
　　　he will serve his parents as his masters.

—Sirach 3:1–7

"Honor your father and your mother, as the LORD your God commanded you; that your days may be prolonged, and that it may go well with you in the land which the LORD your God gives you."

—Deuteronomy 5:16

My son, keep your father's commandment,
    and forsake not your mother's teaching.
Bind them upon your heart always;
    tie them about your neck.
When you walk, they will lead you;
    when you lie down, they will watch over you;
    and when you awake, they will talk with you.
For the commandment is a lamp and the teaching a light,
    and the reproofs of discipline are the way of life. . . .

                        —Proverbs 6: 20–23

Hear, O sons, a father's instruction,
    and be attentive, that you may gain insight;
for I give you good precepts;
    do not forsake my teaching.
When I was a son with my father,
    tender, the only one in the sight of my mother,
he taught me, and said to me,
    "Let your heart hold fast my words;
    keep my commandments, and live."

                        —Proverbs 4: 1–4

My soul takes pleasure in three things,
    and they are beautiful in the sight of the Lord and of
        men:
agreement between brothers, friendship between neighbors,
    and a wife and husband who live in harmony.

                        —Sirach 25: 1

FACE TO FACE WITH JESUS CHRIST

And you he made alive, when you were dead through the
trespasses and sins in which you once walked, following the
course of this world, following the prince of the power of
the air, the spirit that is now at work in the sons of disobedience. Among these we all once lived in the passions of our

flesh, following the desires of body and mind, and so we were by nature children of wrath, like the rest of mankind. But God, who is rich in mercy, out of the great love with which he loved us, even when we were dead through our trespasses, made us alive together with Christ (by grace you have been saved), and raised us up with him, and made us sit with him in the heavenly places in Christ Jesus, that in the coming ages he might show the immeasurable riches of his grace in kindness toward us in Christ Jesus.

—Ephesians 2: 1–7

"A new commandment I give to you, that you love one another; even as I have loved you, that you also love one another. By this all men will know that you are my disciples, if you have love for one another."

—John 13: 34–35

But from there you will seek the LORD your God, and you will find him, if you search after him with all your heart and with all your soul.

—Deuteronomy 4: 29

Finally, all of you, have unity of spirit, sympathy, love of the brethren, a tender heart and a humble mind. Do not return evil for evil or reviling for reviling; but on the contrary bless, for to this you have been called, that you may obtain a blessing.

—1 Peter 3: 8–9

"Again I say to you, if two of you agree on earth about anything they ask, it will be done for them by my Father in heaven. For where two or three are gathered in my name, there am I in the midst of them."

—Matthew 18: 19–20

If I speak in the tongues of men and of angels, but have not love, I am a noisy gong or a clanging cymbal. And if I have prophetic powers, and understand all mysteries and all knowledge, and if

I have all faith, so as to remove mountains, but have not love, I am nothing. If I give away all I have, and if I deliver my body to be burned, but have not love, I gain nothing.

Love is patient and kind; love is not jealous or boastful; it is not arrogant or rude. Love does not insist on its own way; it is not irritable or resentful; it does not rejoice at wrong, but rejoices in the right. Love bears all things, believes all things, hopes all things, endures all things.

Love never ends. . . . So faith, hope, love abide, these three; but the greatest of these is love.

—1 Corinthians 13

Jesus said, "Let the children come to me, and do not hinder them; for to such belongs the kingdom of heaven."

—Matthew 19:14

"Abide in me, and I in you. As the branch cannot bear fruit by itself, unless it abides in the vine, neither can you unless you abide in me. I am the vine, you are the branches. He who abides in me, and I in him, he it is that bears much fruit, for apart from me you can do nothing."

—John 15:4–5

"He who eats my flesh and drinks my blood has eternal life, and I will raise him up at the last day. For my flesh is food indeed, and my blood is drink indeed. He who eats my flesh and drinks my blood abides in me and I in him. As the living Father sent me, and I live because of the Father, so he who eats me will live because of me."

—John 6:54–57

See what love the Father has given us, that we should be called children of God; and so we are.

—1 John 3:1

I have loved you with an everlasting love;
therefore I have continued my faithfulness to you.

—Jeremiah 31:3

Then turning to the disciples he said privately, "Blessed are the eyes which see what you see! For I tell you that many prophets and kings desired to see what you see, and did not see it, and to hear what you hear, and did not hear it."

—*Luke 10:23–24*

"If you abide in me, and my words abide in you, ask whatever you will, and it shall be done for you."

—*John 15:7*

"Hitherto you have asked nothing in my name; ask, and you will receive, that your joy may be full."

—*John 16:24*

JOYFUL PERSEVERANCE

Count it all joy, my brethren, when you meet various trials, for you know that the testing of your faith produces steadfastness. And let steadfastness have its full effect, that you may be perfect and complete, lacking in nothing.

—*James 1:2–4*

Let us not grow weary of doing good, for in due season we shall reap, if we do not lose heart.

—*Galatians 6:9*

The Lord is near to the brokenhearted,
and saves the crushed in spirit.

—*Psalm 34:18*

In this you rejoice, though now for a little while you may have to suffer various trials, so that the genuineness of your faith, more precious than gold which though perishable is tested by fire, may redound to praise and glory and honor at the revelation of Jesus Christ.

—*1 Peter 1:6–7*

. . . the LORD waits to be gracious to you;
    therefore he exalts himself to show mercy to you.
For the LORD is a God of justice;
    blessed are all those who wait for him.

—*Isaiah 30:18*

I will lead the blind
    in a way that they know not,
in paths that they have not known
    I will guide them.
I will turn the darkness before them into light,
    the rough places into level ground.
These are the things I will do,
    and I will not forsake them.

—*Isaiah 42:16*

He will surely be gracious to you at the sound of your cry; when he hears it, he will answer you. And though the Lord give you the bread of adversity and the water of affliction, yet your Teacher will not hide himself any more, but your eyes shall see your Teacher. And your ears shall hear a word behind you, saying, "This is the way, walk in it," when you turn to the right or when you turn to the left.

—*Isaiah 30:20–21*

Yea, thou art my rock and my fortress;
    for thy name's sake lead me and guide me,
take me out of the net which is hidden for me,
    for thou art my refuge.
Into thy hand I commit my spirit;
    thou hast redeemed me, O LORD, faithful God.

—*Psalm 31:3–5*

And after you have suffered a little while, the God of all grace, who has called you to his eternal glory in Christ, will himself restore, establish, and strengthen you. To him be the dominion for ever and ever. Amen.

—*1 Peter 5:10–11*

No temptation has overtaken you that is not common to man. God is faithful, and he will not let you be tempted beyond your strength, but with the temptation will also provide the way of escape, that you may be able to endure it.

—1 Corinthians 10:13

I know how to be abased, and I know how to abound; in any and all circumstances I have learned the secret of facing plenty and hunger, abundance and want. I can do all things in him who strengthens me.

—Philippians 4:12–13

"Behold, I send you out like sheep in the midst of wolves; so be wise as serpents and innocent as doves."

—Matthew 10:16

> The LORD is my light and my salvation;
>   whom shall I fear?
> The LORD is the stronghold of my life;
>   of whom shall I be afraid? . . .
> For he will hide me in his shelter
>   in the day of trouble;
> he will conceal me under the cover of his tent;
>   he will set me high upon a rock.

—Psalm 27:1, 5

He will render to every man according to his works: to those who by patience in well-doing seek for glory and honor and immortality, he will give eternal life.

—Romans 2:6–7

"Fear not, I am the first and the last, and the living one; I died, and behold I am alive for evermore, and I have the keys of Death and Hades."

—Revelation 1:17–18

Be watchful, stand firm in your faith, be courageous, be strong. Let all that you do be done in love.

—*1 Corinthians 16:13–14*

And let us not grow weary in doing good, for in due season we shall reap, if we do not lose heart. So then, as we have opportunity, let us do good to all men, and especially to those who are of the household of faith.

—*Galatians 6:9–10*

Now who is there to harm you if you are zealous for what is right? But even if you do suffer for righteousness' sake, you will be blessed. Have no fear of them, nor be troubled, but in your hearts reverence Christ as Lord. Always be prepared to make a defense to anyone who calls you to account for the hope that is in you, yet do it with gentleness and reverence; and keep your conscience clear, so that, when you are abused, those who revile your good behavior in Christ may be put to shame. For it is better to suffer for doing right, if that should be God's will, than for doing wrong.

—*1 Peter 3:13–17*

For God did not give us a spirit of timidity but a spirit of power and love and self-control.

—*2 Timothy 1:7*

> Godless men utterly deride me,
> but I do not turn away from thy law.

—*Psalm 119:51*

If you are reproached for the name of Christ, you are blessed, because the spirit of glory and of God rests upon you.

—*1 Peter 4:14*

Put to death therefore what is earthly in you: immorality, impurity, passion, evil desire, and covetousness, which is idolatry. On account of these the wrath of God is coming. In these you once walked, when you lived in them. But now put them all away: anger, wrath, malice, slander, and foul talk from your mouth. Do not lie to one another, seeing that you have put off the old nature with its practices and have put on the new nature, which is being renewed in knowledge after the image of its creator.

—*Colossians 3:5–10*

May those who sow in tears
    reap with shouts of joy!
He that goes forth weeping,
    bearing the seed for sowing,
shall come home with shouts of joy,
    bringing his sheaves with him.

—*Psalm 126:5–6*

I sought the LORD, and he answered me,
    and delivered me from all my fears.
Look to him, and be radiant;
    so your faces shall never be ashamed.

—*Psalm 34:4–5*

Have you sinned, my son? Do no more,
    but pray about your former sins.
Flee from sin as from a snake;
    for if you approach sin, it will bite you.
Its teeth are lion's teeth,
    and destroy the souls of men.
All lawlessness is like a two-edged sword;
    there is no healing for its wound.
Terror and violence will lay waste riches;
    thus the house of the proud will be laid waste.

—*Sirach 21:1–4*

My soul drew near to death,
    and my life was very near to Hades beneath.
They surrounded me on every side,
    and there was no one to help me;

96

I looked for the assistance of men,
and there was none.
Then I remembered thy mercy, O Lord,
and thy work from of old,
that thou dost deliver those who wait for thee
and dost save them from the hand of their enemies.

—Sirach 51:6–8

"Ask, and it will be given you; seek, and you will find; knock, and it will be opened to you. For everyone who asks receives, and he who seeks finds, and to him who knocks it will be opened. For what man of you, if his son asks him for bread, will give him a stone? Or if he asks for a fish, will give him a serpent? If you then, who are evil, know how to give good gifts to your children, how much more will your Father who is in heaven give good things to those who ask him!"

—Matthew 7:7–11

Then the king will say to those at his right hand, "Come, O blessed of my Father, inherit the kingdom prepared for you from the foundation of the world."

—Matthew 25:34

"They shall hunger no more, neither thirst any more;
the sun shall not strike them, nor any scorching heat.
For the Lamb in the midst of the throne will be their
shepherd,
and he will guide them to springs of living water;
and God will wipe away every tear from their eyes."

—Revelation 7:16–17

We know that we are of God, and the whole world is in the power of the evil one. And we know that the Son of God has come and has given us understanding, to know him who is true; and we are in him who is true, in his Son Jesus Christ. This is the true God and eternal life. Little children, keep yourselves from idols.

—1 John 5:19–21

"Then the righteous will shine like the sun in the kingdom of their Father. He who has ears, let him hear."

—*Matthew 13:43*

So we do not lose heart. Though our outer nature is wasting away, our inner nature is being renewed every day. For this slight momentary affliction is preparing for us an eternal weight of glory beyond all comparison, because we look not to the things that are seen but to the things that are unseen; for the things that are seen are transient, but the things that are unseen are eternal.

—*2 Corinthians 4:16–18*

And when the chief Shepherd is manifested, you will obtain the unfading crown of glory.

—*1 Peter 5:4*

But, as it is written,
"What no eye has seen, nor ear heard,
nor the heart of man conceived,
what God has prepared for those who love him,"
God has revealed to us through the Spirit.

—*1 Corinthians 2:9–10*

The Lord watches over the sojourners,
he upholds the widow and the fatherless;
but the way of the wicked he brings to ruin.

—*Psalm 146:9*

And I am sure that he who began a good work in you will bring it to completion at the day of Jesus Christ.

—*Philippians 1:6*

If we confess our sins, he is faithful and just, and will forgive our sins and cleanse us from all unrighteousness. If we say we have not sinned, we make him a liar, and his word is not in us.

—*1 John 1:9–10*

If you turn to him with all your heart and with all your soul,
    to do what is true before him,
then he will turn to you
    and will not hide his face from you.
But see what he will do with you;
    give thanks to him with your full voice.

               —*Tobit 13:6*

I have swept away your transgressions like a cloud,
    and your sins like mist;
return to me, for I have redeemed you.

               —*Isaiah 44:22*

Blessed is he whose transgression is forgiven,
    whose sin is covered.
Blessed is the man to whom the LORD imputes no iniquity,
    and in whose spirit there is no deceit.

When I declared not my sin, my body wasted away
    through my groaning all day long.
For day and night your hand was heavy upon me;
    my strength was dried up as by the heat of summer.

I acknowledged my sin to thee,
    and I did not hide my iniquity;
I said, "I will confess my transgressions to the LORD";
    then thou didst forgive the guilt of my sin.

               —*Psalm 32:1–5*

He has delivered us from the dominion of darkness and transferred us to the kingdom of his beloved Son, in whom we have redemption, the forgiveness of sins.

               —*Colossians 1:13–14*

There is no fear in love, but perfect love casts out fear. For fear has to do with punishment, and he who fears is not perfected in love. We love because he first loved us.

               —*1 John 4:18–19*

Behold, God is my salvation;
    I will trust, and will not be afraid;
for the Lord God is my strength and my song,
    and he has become my salvation.

With joy you will draw water from the wells of salvation.

—Isaiah 12:2–3

    For I, the Lord your God,
        hold your right hand;
    it is I who say to you, "Fear not,
        I will help you."

—Isaiah 41:13

For the mountains may depart
    and the hills be removed,
but my steadfast love shall not depart from you,
    and my covenant of peace shall not be removed,
says the Lord, who has compassion on you.

—Isaiah 54:10

    Cast your burden on the Lord,
        and he will sustain you;
    he will never permit
        the righteous to be disturbed.

—Psalm 55:23

The Lord is near to all who call upon him
    to all who call upon him in truth.
He fulfills the desire of all who fear him;
    he hears their cry, and saves them.

—Psalm 145:18–19

He only is my rock and my salvation,
    my fortress; I shall not be shaken.
On God rests my deliverance and my honor;
    my mighty rock, my refuge is God.

—Psalm 62:6–8

Behold, God is my helper;
the Lord is the upholder of my life.

—Psalm 54:4

"Let not your hearts be troubled; believe in God; believe also in me."

—John 14:1

For thou, O Lord, art my hope,
my trust, O Lord, from my youth.

—Psalm 71:5

Who ever trusted in the Lord and was put to shame? . . .
Or who ever called upon him and was overlooked?
For the Lord is compassionate and merciful;
he forgives sins and saves in time of affliction.

—Sirach 2:10–11

Blessed be the God and Father of our Lord Jesus Christ, the Father of mercies and God of all comfort, who comforts us in all our affliction, so that we may be able to comfort those who are in any affliction, with the comfort with which we ourselves are comforted by God. For as we share abundantly in Christ's sufferings, so through Christ we share abundantly in comfort too.

—2 Corinthians 1:3–5

But the Lord is faithful; he will strengthen you and guard you from evil.

—2 Thessalonians 3:3

We know that in everything God works for good with those who love him, who are called according to his purpose.

—Romans 8:28

. . for whatever is born of God overcomes the world. And this is the victory that overcomes the world, our faith.

—1 John 5:4

Therefore do not throw away your confidence, which has a great reward. For you have need of endurance, so that you may do the will of God and receive what is promised.

—Hebrews 10:35–36

Have I not commanded you? Be strong and of good courage; be not frightened, neither be dismayed; for the Lord your God is with you wherever you go.

—Joshua 1:9

> Nevertheless I am continually with thee;
> Thou dost hold my right hand.
> Thou dost guide me with they counsel,
> and afterward thou wilt receive me to glory.

—Psalm 73:23–24

No, in all these things we are more than conquerors through him who loved us. For I am sure that neither death, nor life, nor angels, nor principalities, nor things present, nor things to come, nor powers, nor height, nor depth, nor anything else in all creation, will be able to separate us from the love of God in Christ Jesus our Lord.

—Romans 8:37–39

Let us hold fast to the confession of our hope without wavering, for he who promised is faithful.

—Hebrews 10:23

> "Can a woman forget her sucking child,
> that she should have no compassion on the son of her
> womb?"
> Even these may forget,
> yet I will not forget you.
> Behold, I have graven you on the palms of my hands;
> your walls are continually before me.

—Isaiah 49:15–16

"Fear not, little flock, for it is your Father's good pleasure to give you the kingdom."

—Luke 12:32

> But the righteous live forever,
> and their reward is with the Lord;
> the Most High takes care of them.
> Therefore they will receive a glorious crown
> and a beautiful diadem from the hand of the Lord,
> because with his right hand he will cover them,
> and with his arm he will shield them.

—Wisdom 5:15–16

Rejoice in the Lord always; again I will say, Rejoice. Let all men know your forbearance. The Lord is at hand. Have no anxiety about anything, but in everything by prayer and supplication with thanksgiving let your requests be made known to God. And the peace of God, which passes all understanding, will keep your hearts and your minds in Christ Jesus.

—Philippians 4:4–7